CAMPFIRE LEGENDS

Edited by John Long

ICS BOOKS, Inc.
Merrillville, IN

CAMPFIRE LEGENDS

Copyright © 1993 by John Long

10 9 8 7 6 5 4 3 2 1

Printed in the U.S.A.

To Marjohnny Lorine, chiquita, blanquita, e linda.

Published by:
ICS Books, Inc.
1370 E. 87th Place
Merrillville, IN 46410
800-541-7323

Library of Congress Cataloging-in-Publication Data

Campfire legends / edited by John Long
      p. cm.
     Includes index.
     ISBN 0-934802-16-5 : $9.99
     1. Literature--Collections.   I. Long, John, 1954-
PN6014.c28   1993
808.8--dc20
                        93-26008
                           CIP

Perhaps there are still trails leading to mystery and danger waiting to be discovered in some distant range—trails, maybe, like this one.

INTRODUCTION

Nowhere on earth do the stories fly as when friends are gathered around a fire. Roll in a little fog, rustle the limbs a bit and the very Pope will "remember" stories that Baalim's ass couldn't begin to swallow. Give credit to the fire itself, which charms the eyes and burns away the chatter in our minds. At the fireside we feel alone, which makes us antsy, imposing on us a void begging to be filled not with just any story, but with one that either amplifies the solitude, or shatters it altogether. This is traditionally accomplished with highly imagined yarns—but not always.

Take Virginia Reed's letter to her cousin, written in 1846 when she was 13 years old, describing how she and her family joined the Donner-Reed party on its doomed journey to California. The child Reed summarizes this fabled American tragedy with such guileless, naked honesty that if you got someone with one of those bottom-of-the-well voices to read it aloud, it could raise goosebumps on a granite frieze. Still, I've never believed that a thorough scare is the only viable camp-fire story, so I haven't checked Legends by that formula. Soft-pedaled masterpieces like Castro Z's "Lucero," and Borges' "The Book of Mark," show that a gentle stroke, artfully directed, can hit the mark as sure as a sledge hammer. Feeling that a little humor can add a lot, I've couched the longer stories between short pieces that came from a wide variety of sources.

If you're ever around a campfire, Legends might come in handy. I've found these pages no less valuable on crowded planes, in strange hotel rooms, or during those blue funks when I'm moping around myu own place, too annoyed to sit down and plough through something "important." Here, I need a quick shot, something to clear the decks; and my boredom and anxieties have never stood a chance against these pages.

At least half of these stories are literary classics, and are best appreciated in a quiet, well lighted room. Because the light at a campfire is often lacking, I've included a short, large-print summary at the end of each story to help guide a raconteur if he/she is pressed into telling the stories from memory, or if the light will simply not allow a word-by-word telling. To do justice to these stories you can't miss a word, because much of the artistry and charm is in the execution. But at the very least, using the summaries will provide the framework for a fine tale, and will hopefully get listeners to go back and read the complete stories in more favorable conditions.

I'd like to believe many of these stories sprang straight from the fire itself. For certain, they are best enjoyed around one (be it in your living room or Madagascar), where far above the stars glare down like the eyes of a staring crowd, as if the whole universe awaits the next story. Yo-ho-ho and a bottle of rum!

John Long
Valencia, Venezuela

TABLE OF CONTENTS

CREDITS

1. John Lutz, *Tough* from *Black Lizard Anthology of Crime*, © John Lutz, Dominick Abel Literary Agency, Inc. Reprinted by permission.

2. "The Gospel According to Mark" from *Doctor Brodie's Report* by Jorge Luis Borges. Copyright (c) 1970, 1971, 1972 by Emece Editores, S.A., and Norman Thomas di Giovanni. Used by permission of Dutton Signet, a division of Penguin Books USA Inc.

3. From a letter by Judge Roy "Tall" Cotten to his brother, Amarillo, Texas, 1873. *Humor of the American Cowboy,* Caxton Printers, Ltd.

4. From *Humor of the American Cowboy* by Stan Hoig, © 1958 Caxton Printers, Ltd.

5. "The Adventures of Sidi-Nouman" from the *Arabian Nights Entertainment,* selected and edited by Andrew Lang. Reprinted by permission of Dover Publications, Inc.

6. "Fauna of the United States" from *The Book of Imaginary Beings* by Jorge Luis Borges with Margarita Guerrero, translated by Norman Thomas di Giovanni. Translation copyright (c) 1969 by Jorge Luis Borges and Norman Thomas di Giovanni. Used by permission of Dutton Signet, a division of Penguin Books USA Inc.

7. From *Humor of the American Cowboy* by Stan Hoig, © 1958 Caxton Printers, Ltd.

8. From *The Short Stories of Katherine Mansfield* by Katherine Mansfield. Copyright 1924 by Alfred A. Knopf, Inc., and renewed 1952 by J. Middleton Murry. Reprinted by permission of the publisher.

9. "Where There's a Will" by Richard Matheson and Richard Christian Matheson from *Dark Forces* edited by Kirby McCauley.

10. "The End of the Duel," from *Doctor Brodie's Report* by Jorge Luis Borges. Copyright (c) 1970, 1971, 1972 by Emece Editores, S.A., and Norman Thomas di Giovanni. Used by permission of Dutton Signet, a division of Penguin Books USA Inc.

11. "The Sphinx," from *The Book of Imaginary Beings* by Jorge Luis Borges with Margarita Guerrero, translated by Norman Thomas di Giovanni. Translation copyright (c) 1969 by Jorge Luis Borges and Norman Thomas di Giovanni. Used by permission of Dutton Signet, a division of Penguin Books USA Inc.

12. Ninth tale of *The Decameron* by Boccaccio. © The Estate of Richard Aldington.

13. "Enemies" from *The Things They Carried* by Tim O'Brien. Copyright (c) 1990 by Tim O'Brien. Reprinted by permission of Houghton Mifflin Co./Seymour Lawrence. All rights reserved.

TOUGH

by John Lutz

Metzger watched through his old army binoculars as the car veered from the main highway that was barely visible as a distant, faint ribbon on the surface of the desert. A lazy plume of dust rose and hung in the air like a signal, telling Metzger that the car was on the old fork road, heading his way.

A lean, sun-browned man somewhere between fifty and seventy years of age, Metzger put down his binoculars, rubbed his gray and gritty beard and frowned. He lived alone, and he spent a lot of his time here at the window, watching the highway. His shack was one of fifteen deserted and dilapidated clapboard structures that were the remains of hippies' commune of the mid-Sixties. Metzger had lived nearby then, near a rise on the other side of the highway, and when the last of the commune people had left, he moved into the best of the shacks and the one with the clearest view of the faraway highway that was his one link with his fellow man.

He again raised the binoculars to his pale blue eyes. The car was only a few miles away now. Judging by the size of the dust cloud it raised, it was a big car.

The three men in the gray Lincoln sedan were cool despite the desert's ninety-eight-degree temperature. The car's powerful air-condi-tioner was more than a match for the late afternoon sun. All three men wore dark expensive suits and were neatly groomed. The two in the front seat were in their late thirties. The third man, Eddie Hastings, a dark-haired classically handsome man with white, even teeth and a curiously jaunty demeanor, was in his twenties. But Eddie considered himself tough enough for this company or any company. He had held up his end of the job back in Vegas, which was one reason why they were driving now with more than half a million dollars of stolen casino money in the trunk. It was Vito Dellano, the car's driver, who had shot the man giving chase in the casino's parking lot. Eddie knew that the man had posed no real threat. Vito had shot him because he felt mean at the moment. Plenty of reason for Vito.

The other man in the front seat provided a study in opposites. He was short while Vito Dellano was tall; fair while Vito was dark; blond and curly-haired while Vito was black-haired and approaching baldness. His name was Art Grogan. He had been an enforcer and bodyguard in the eastern mob for the last ten years. He had met Eddie Hastings during a brief stint in prison more than a year ago, and the plan was born.

Vito provided the in they needed at the casino, and early this morning they had made the biggest score of their criminal lives, a dream score.

Now they needed to lie low for awhile, divide the holdup proceeds, and then anonymously begin new lives. They had developed car trouble, a leaking oil line, a few miles back, and when they'd spotted the distant cluster of shacks from a rise in the highway, they'd decided to conceal the car and themselves there and wait out the inevitable manhunt. Vito remembered the place from years ago. They were sharp, mean and Big City all the way. No one would expect them to hole up in a remote and crude desert ruin.

Metzger saw the three men and felt a sudden dread. They had spotted his run-down Jeep and parked near it. He could hear them talking.

"You think this heap actually runs?" the hulking dark one said.

"The point is," a dapper, good-looking youngster answered, "it belongs to someone. It ain't been here forever like the rest of these junkers. See how you can still make out its tire tracks in the sand?"

All three men gazed through shimmering desert air toward the nearest of the canted clapboard shacks, toward Metzger's home. The men glanced at one another, and then they spread out as if on military maneuver and advanced on the shack.

Metzger quickly gathered up his boots, knife and a canteen of water and made for the back door.

But when he opened the door the blond man was standing outside smiling at him. He was holding a revolver.

"It ain't hospitable to run out on your guests," he said, motioning with the gun for Metzger to go back inside. Metzger obeyed and the blond man followed.

"Were you goin' somewhere?" Eddie asked in an amused voice. "An important appointment, maybe?"

"So's we understand each other right off," Vito said, and stepped over and backhanded Metzger viciously across the face.

Metzger, backing away in a scurry of scrawny brown limbs, almost fell down. He raised a hand and felt blood on his lean cheekbone.

"Nice place you got here," Grogan said with a chuckle. He patted an errant lock of blond hair into place with his free hand and glanced around. "We're gonna be staying here for awhile, old man. That is, if you invite us."

Metzger stood silently, staring at the bare wood floor. He had a radio in the shack. They would notice it, soon, know that he might have heard about the casino robbery on the news. Three well-dressed men in a big car. Who else could they be? And they had killed a casino employee.

Vito stepped near enough to hit Metzger again if he so chose.

"Stay as long as you like," Metzger muttered, still staring at the floor.

"Very neighborly," Eddie remarked. He walked around, opened doors. "Hey, looka here, a freezer. Not big, but there's meat in it."

"No TV, though," Grogan said, "But look if it ain't a radio."

"You listen to the radio much, old man?" Vito asked.

Metzger shrugged ebony shoulders.

"He knows," Grogan said. He absently twisted the large diamond ring he liked to flash. The ring was on the trigger finger of the hand holding the revolver. "Not that it makes any difference."

"How often do you go into town for supplies?" Eddie asked Metzger.

"Every few months." The voice was a quaking whisper.

How the hell do you live on just that?"

"I hunt."

Vito smiled. "Check around for a rifle, Eddie."

Eddie found the gun almost immediately, a modified old Enfield army rifle. "An antique," he said. "Like its owner."

"It looks to me like it'd fire," Grogan said. "That's what counts." He frowned and looked around at the bare walls, the glassless windows and the sink that supported a bucket of greenish well water. "How long do you figure we'll—"

Something suddenly rammed into Grogan. It was Vito. Grogan caught a glimpse of a fleeting shadow, tried to raise the gun in his hand. His wrist struck Vito's arm and the shot hammered harmlessly into the wood floor. Eddie, who was standing on the other side of the room, stared slack-mouthed at the window through which the old man had disappeared. It was almost as if the bearded desert creature had been an illusion. He'd been here; he was gone. Like that.

Vito cursed angrily. Then he smiled. He laughed. "He was laying back on us, the old bastard! He wasn't half so scared as he pretended. He was just waitin' his chance."

"He was quick when it come," Eddie said. "So quick I hardly seen him make it out the window."

"He's an old sand rabbit," Vito said, still grinning. "What do you expect? But there ain't no place he can go. Let's spread out and search all these shacks."

Guns at the ready, the three men from Las Vegas, sweating now and in shirt sleeves, began a systematic search of the ramshackle ruins.

Metzger was under the floor of the shack near the center of the old commune, in the dug-out space where once drugs had been hidden. He knew they would search for him, and before long they came. He lay perfectly still and listened to the cautious hollow footsteps overhead, saw the indistinguishable shape through the cracks in the floor boards. Then the searcher, satisfied that the shack was empty, moved on.

Metzger laughed soundlessly. He had caught them off guard, pretended that he was scared nearly numb. But he had sized up the three men almost immediately. Tough. City tough. But Metzger hadn't survived Korea, then all these years alone in the desert, by being soft.

"I don't get it," Eddie said, forearming perspiration from his face. "He ain't in any of the shacks, so where did he go?"

Vito licked cracked lips and swiveled his head to take in the spread of weathered, leaning shacks. "Oh, he's still here somewhere."

"He ain't armed," Grogan said wearily. "He can't harm us none, and he ain't goin' to—" He suddenly raised a hand to his chin. "The Jeep!"

"Relax," Vito said through his wide grin. He held up a ring of keys. "I took these before we started lookin' for the old coot. And I took the distributor caps as well from both the Jeep and the Lincoln. He ain't goin' nowhere. Which gives me an idea."

The three men returned to Metzger's shack. Vito decided he would take Metzger's Jeep and drive it to the crest of a distant rise. He had noticed a pair of binoculars in the shack, and on top of the rise he would be able to sit and use them to scan the array of run down structures until he saw some sign of the old man. He would note the location carefully, drive back to join the others, and then they would deal with their unexpectedly elusive quarry.

Vito took the binoculars, a canteen full of the brackish well water, and after making the ancient army surplus Jeep serviceable, he set off in the midst of the rattles, exhaust fumes and dust toward the distant rise of sand that shimmered in dancing heat waves. Eddie and Grogan hurried back into the dim comparative coolness of the shack's interior.

Less than an hour had passed when something came hurtling through the window and landed with a thump on the floor near Eddie. He yelled and jumped, unconsciously drawing his automatic from its shoulder holster. But the object on the floor was only something small and wrapped in a dirty gray rag.

Grogan came over to stand by Eddie, and both men stared down at the lump of cloth. Then Eddie felt a sudden anger at himself for letting the crazy old coot startle him. He knelt and carefully unwrapped the cloth.

"It's just a rock," Grogan said, watching studiously.

"Yeah," Eddie replied. Then he straightened violently. "Holy Mother!"

Grogan was staring wide-eyed at him, puzzled. "What is it?" And then he saw.

"It's a finger. . ." Eddie said. "It's somebody's cut-off finger."

Both men knelt and stared at the small putty-colored digit in the dirty cloth. It appeared to be a man's little finger. Grogan had seen something like it before when Larry Collissimo had been blown up in his car in St. Louis.

"A note," Eddie said, and he unfolded the slip of paper that had been in the cloth-wrapped package with the rock and bloodless finger.

"He's got Vito," he said in a flat voice after reading the scrawled note. "He says come now—just one of us—to the shack farthest west and trade his finger for Vito, or he'll give us the rest of Vito as dead as Vito's little finger."

Grogan was pale even for Grogan. His shirt was plastered to his short, muscular torso. He grinned a predator's grin. "He'll want all of our weapons and our car keys," he said. "And who knows what else? You know, you almost gotta admire the old bastard."

"Remember, he's got Vito's gun now," Eddie said. "And the Jeep. Why do you figure he just didn't up and run?"

"How far would he get in that ratty old Jeep with us after him?" Grogan asked. "Or maybe he ain't got enough gas to get anywhere. Anyway, we'll just go see him."

"He said just one of us," Eddie cautioned.

"Just one of us will go to the front of the shack," Grogan said. "You'll be coming up from the other direction."

"What about Vito?"

"We'll save him if we can."

The men stared at each other, both thinking about half a million dollars split two ways instead of three. They checked their weapons and left the shack.

As he doubled around to approach the rear of the shack where the old man waited, Eddie glanced at the ridge Vito had started out for. He could see nothing but blazing, lowering sun. All around him the desert was starkly shadowed and eerily desolate, wavering in the heat, with deep purples and reds cast over its undulating surface. Eddie spat, mustered his determination and cautiously moved forward.

"Old man!" Grogan called, when he was within fifty feet of the shack's half-hinged front door.

There was no answer. Grogan hefted his revolver and continued toward the shack.

A snap, a whir, a cloud of sand at Grogan's feet.

At first he thought he'd been bitten by a rattlesnake. Then he stared with amazement at the knife protruding from his chest. The old man had rigged some kind of spring trap, concealed it beneath the sand. A supple length of wire was lashed to the knife's handle and attached to something on the ground.

Breathing hoarsely, fighting the pain, Grogan fastened his fingers about the knife and slowly removed it. As it slid free, he screamed. He took three steps, whimpered and fell.

Eddie heard Grogan scream. Crouched low, he ran toward the front of the shack. In the distorting purple shadows, he almost fell over Grogan.

He glanced toward the shack. "Damn him!" he moaned. He grabbed Grogan's revolver before running for cover.

Eddie had had enough of the old man. The thing to do now was to get in the Lincoln, leaky oil line or not, and get as far away as possible.

As he reached the old man's shack, Eddie stopped and stood still, panting, feeling spasms of confusion and fear. The Jeep was parked alongside the Lincoln.

The shack's door opened and Vito stepped out onto the plank porch.

He glowered at Eddie. "Where the hell is Grogan?" he asked.

Eddie trudged forward, a gun in each hand, his shoulders slumped. "Grogan's dead," he said. He stared at Vito's hands.

Metzger sat leaning against the rough wall and expertly adjusted the bandage about the stump of the severed little finger of his left hand. He was grinning through the pain, his teeth crooked and yellow in his sun-darkened face. He had bagged one. If he could have grabbed the fallen one's gun, he'd have gotten two of the intruders. But the young one had been too quick for Metzger this time.

Metzger heard the Jeep drive away, watched it disappear in the direction of the ridge. He knew what their plan was, so he devised one of his own. Easy enough to stay out of sight. And a little finger was fair trade for his life. His idea had been worth a try and partially successful.

Sweat streamed down Metzger's lean face into his matted beard, but he didn't mind the heat. He had been frostbitten at the Chosin Reservoir in Korea. After living through that fiercest of battles and retreats, he had vowed never to be cold, hungry and afraid again. So after his discharge he had come to the desert and never once had he minded the heat or desolation. He knew how to get by in the inhospitable desert. He had learned how years ago from a uranium prospector who had befriended him.

"The old codger's tougher than we thought," Vito said, after Eddie explained what had happened. Vito had been driving back from the ridge when the confrontation took place.

"I say we climb in the car and get out," Eddie said.

"And leave the old bastard alive? There ain't that many turn-offs in this part of the country. No place to hide. If the cops come by here and talk to him, we'll be caught in a few hours. First we take care of the old man, then we leave."

"What's you see from the ridge?" Eddie asked.

"Nothin'. He's stayin' holed up." Vito's dark brows lowered. "I did run into somethin' odd, though. A junkyard of old cars half buried in the sun. Must be dozens of 'em."

"Spare parts!" Eddie said. "Maybe we can fix the oil line!"

"I got a better suggestion," Vito said. "We siphon the gas outa the Lincoln, put it in the Jeep and take that. When we leave, the old man won't be in any condition to report it stolen."

Eddie silently chewed on the inside of his cheek. The old man. The rickety desert rat who couldn't weigh more than a hundred and forty pounds. He was proving to be a surprisingly difficult obstacle to overcome. And Eddie knew that Vito was right. In order for them to get away clean, the old man had to die. Eddie looked out the nearest window and saw that the desert was almost dark. Stars seemed to be staring down from the night sky like the eyes of animals. "Any ideas?" he asked Vito.

"One'll come," he assured him. "Here's the situation. We can't leave the old man, and he can't leave because he's got no wheels. That highway might be visible, but it's almost fifteen hard miles away—too far for an old heart-attack risk like that to walk to in the desert either by day or by night."

"So it's a stand off," Eddie said.

Vito turned on a lamp fashioned from an old glass jug. "Not to my way of thinking," he said. "We've got food and water here. The old man might be able to find water, but not food."

Just then, the light flickered and went out, and Vito and Eddie heard the freezer motor waver then gurgle to silence.

"Wait here!" Vito commanded. He went outside, got a flashlight from the glove compartment of the Lincoln and shone it about the exterior of the shack, playing the flashlight beam along the ground in front of him. He didn't want to die the way Eddie said Grogan had died.

Eddie waited nervously for almost fifteen minutes before hearing footsteps on the front porch. He was backed into a corner, his gun drawn, when the door opened and the faint moonlight revealed the unmistakable bulk of Vito.

"He's busted up the generator for keeps," Vito said.

"Then we're even up with the old man," Eddie said. "That meat in the freezer will spoil in no time. We gotta leave."

Vito stood scowling, occasionally wiping sweat from his thick brows. He knew Eddie was right, but he didn't like admitting that a whiskey old man had outsmarted them. But if they were going to leave, it might as well be as soon as possible and under cover of darkness.

"You keep an eye out for the old coyote," Vito said. "I'll siphon the gas from the Jeep and transfer the money."

Eddie nodded, wondering if the old man had recovered his knife from Grogan's dead hand. He didn't like this a bit, not in the dark.

But Eddie had no reason to worry about night-time sentry duty. Vito returned and told him that the tires on both the Jeep and the Lincoln had been slashed. Now hunter and prey were equally immobile. And there was something else about the slashed tires that sent a shiver of doubt and stifled terror through Eddie.

The old man didn't want them to leave. He had gone on the offensive.

Eddie cooked some partially spoiled ground beef that first night and again for breakfast. But by the second afternoon the rest of the meat in the now-hot freezer smelled strongly and was unfit to eat. At least Eddie and Vito were one day up on the old man. He hadn't eaten since yesterday morning.

The electric pump that drew water from the well was useless now, so they rationed the water in the bucket in the sink. There was plenty of it. But water proved a poor substitute for food. Eddie hadn't been hungry since his boyhood in Brooklyn, and he'd never been this hungry.

By the fourth day, Vito and Eddie did little but slump in opposite corners of the shack and endure the hunger and the heat. They no longer tried to even talk. Eddie was sure that the old man must be dead by now, but he was too weak to care. They could only hope that someone would see the distant dots of the shacks from the highway, as Vito did, and make the mistake of driving over to investigate.

By late afternoon Eddie wondered if he might be hallucinating. He decided that he was only drifting in and out of sleep because of his weakened condition. But he dreamed, and the dreams were so real. Like this one. He could swear that the old man was standing before him, stacking all the weapons on a table. And Vito was sitting up in a chair, tied to it with a thick rope. And Eddie was sitting up also. He suddenly knew that he wasn't dreaming at all. The old man was grinning down at him.

Eddie fought against the ropes that held him. Even at his strongest he wouldn't have been able to budge. He squinted at the old man and saw that he seemed to be none the worse for his ordeal. In fact, he appeared more well fed and healthy than when they had first seen him.

"The old bastard tricked us," Vito said weakly but with venom.

The gray-bearded man in front of Eddie smiled acknowledgement for the compliment. Grogan's diamond ring glinted on his scrawny middle finger. The stub of the little finger of the same hand was still neatly wrapped.

"What'd you eat?" Eddie asked, "Cactus?"

"That's where I got my water," the old man said. "I et meat."

"But where?. . ." A coldness suddenly spiraled through Eddie. He realized where the old man had gotten meat. He understood now, too, about the "junkyard" Vito had seen. He knew how the old man survived way out here alone in the vast, cruel desert.

"You get them from the highway, don't you?" Eddie asked.

"Ever once in a great while," the old man said. "Often as I need."

Vito squirmed helplessly in his chair. "What the hell are you two talkin' about?"

"Look at him," Eddie said, "and think about that junkyard of cars you saw. Think about Grogan."

"I still don't get it."

"He killed Grogan and lived off his body while we were starving."

Vito stared at the old man with horror, then he began to laugh crazily, the whites of his eyes glittering.

When he was finished laughing, he looked at Eddie and actually winked. He was Big Vito again. "Don't let it get to you, kid. Our string's run out, that's all. When you're dead you're dead, and it don't matter what happens to the meat."

Eddie suddenly fixed wide eyes on the useless freezer and then on the old man. Something had occurred to him. "If Grogan was dead," he said, "How did you keep him from. . ."

"That was a problem I learned how to handle some years back," the old man said. He looked at Eddie and waited.

"Oh, dear God!" Eddie croaked.

"Your friend Grogan had passed out and lost a mite of blood, that's all," the old man said.

Eddie's face was contorted, his mouth open as if he were screaming, but the scream was soundless.

Vito stared at him, still not understanding. But he would understand.

"Now we'll see how tough you really are," the old man said. And he untied Vito's left arm.

SUMMARY:

1. A lean, desert-hardened old man (Metzger) watches as three other men drive their Lincoln toward his dilapidated desert commune outside of Las Vegas. The three men have pulled off a casino heist, and now Eddie, Vito and Grogan are looking for a place to hole up. They settle on the group of shacks where the old man lives.

2. The Lincoln parks next to the old man's Jeep, and the three men descend on the old man's house, cornering him just before he can escape. They pull a gun on him. First they notice his freezer, which is stocked with meat, then his radio. They know now that the old man knows who they are and what they've done.

3. Suddenly, the old man breaks free, flinging Vito, his captor, into Grogan. In a flash, he disappears out the window of the shack, leaving Eddie to wonder if he were just an illusion.

4. The three search the shacks, but can't find the old man, who has hidden beneath the floor of one of them. Vito decides to take the old man's Jeep and scout the area; Grogan and Eddie are waiting in the shack when an object hurtles through the window. It is a severed finger, with a note that says the old man has Vito.

5. Eddie and Grogan go to the shack where the old man is hiding. As Grogan approaches, he feels an odd sensation, then notices a knife protruding from his chest. Eddie runs back to the old man's shack, only to find Vito waiting for him.

6. Eddie and Vito decide they must kill the old man before they leave the desert compound. They wait, eating the old man's meat and drinking his water. They figure Metzger is starving.

7. Metzger cuts off the power, so the pump for the well won't run and the meat in the freezer spoils, and slashes the tires on the Jeep and the Lincoln.

8. On the fourth day without food or water, the old man creeps back into the shack and ties up Eddie and Vito.

9. Eddie marvels that the old man appears well fed—then it dawns on him. The old man has eaten Grogan to stay alive. But how, he wonders, did the old man keep the meat from spoiling?

10. The answer to that question becomes clear as the old man unties one of Vito's arms.

ON BOARD THE DERELICT

Young E. Allison

Fifteen men on the dead man's chest—
  "Yo-ho-ho and a bottle of rum!
"Drink and the devil had done for the rest—
  "Yo-ho-ho and a bottle of rum!"
The mate was fixed by the bos'n's pike,
The bos'n brained with a marlinspike
And Cookey's throat was marked belike.
    It had been gripped
    By fingers ten;
    And there they lay,
    All good dead men,
Like break-o'-day in a boozing-ken—
  Yo-ho-ho and a bottle of rum!

Fifteen men of a whole ship's list—
  Yo-ho-ho and a bottle of rum!
Dead and bedamned and the rest gone whist!—
  Yo-ho-ho and a bottle of rum!
The skipper lay with his nob in gore
Where the scullion's axe his cheek had shore—
And the scullion he was stabbed times four.
    And there they lay
    And the soggy skies
    Dripped all day long
    In up-staring eyes—
At murk sunset and at foul sunrise—
  Yo-ho-ho and a bottle of rum!

Fifteen men of 'em stiff and stark—
  Yo-ho-ho and a bottle of rum!
Ten of the crew had the Murder mark—
  Yo-ho-ho and a bottle of rum!

'Twas a cutlass swipe, or an ounce of lead,
Or a yawning hole in a battered head—
And the scuppers glut with a rotting red.
    And there they lay—
    Aye, damn my eyes!—
    All lookouts clapped
    On paradise—
All souls bound contrariwise—
    Yo-ho-ho and a bottle of rum!

Fifteen men of 'em good and true—
    Yo-ho-ho and a bottle of rum!
Every man jack could ha' sailed with Old Pew—
    Yo-ho-ho and a bottle of rum!
There was chest on chest of Spanish gold,
With a ton of plate in the middle hold,
And the cabins riot of stuff untold,
    And they lay there,
    That had took the plum,
    With sightless glare
    And their tongues struck dumb,
While we shared all by the rule of thumb—
    Yo-ho-ho and a bottle of rum!

More was seen through the sternlit screen—
    Yo-ho-ho and a bottle of rum!
A flimsy shift on a bunker cot,
With a thin red slot through the bosom spot
And the lace stiff-dry in a purplish blot.
    Or was she a wench,
    Or some shuddering maid?
    That dared the knife—
    And that took the blade!
By God! she was stuff for a plucky jade—
    Yo-ho-ho and a bottle of rum!

"Fifteen men on a dead man's chest—
    "Yo-ho-ho and a bottle of rum!

15

"Drink and the devil had done for the rest—
  "Yo-ho-ho and a bottle of rum!"
We wrapped 'em all in a mains'l tight,
With twice ten turns of a howser's bight,
And we heaved 'em over and out of sight—
  With a yo-heave-ho!
  And a fare-you-well!
  And a sullen plunge
  In the sullen swell
Ten fathoms deep on the road to hell!
  Yo-ho-ho and a bottle of rum!

THE GOSPEL ACCORDING TO MARK

by Jorge Luis Borges

These events took place at La Colorada ranch, in the southern part of the township of Junin, during the last days of March, 1928. The protagonist was a medical student named Baltasar Espinosa. We may describe him, for now, as one of the common run of young men from Buenos Aires, with nothing more noteworthy about him than an almost unlimited kindness and a capacity for public speaking that had earned him several prizes at the English school in Ramos Mejia. He did not like arguing, and preferred having his listener rather than himself in the right. Although he was fascinated by the probabilities of chance in any game he played, he was a bad player because it gave him no pleasure to win. His wide intelligence was undirected; at the age of thirty-three, he still lacked credit for graduation, by one course—the course to which he was most drawn. His father, who was a freethinker (like all the gentlemen of his day), had introduced him to the lessons of Herbert Spencer, but his mother, before leaving him on a trip to Montevideo, once asked him to say the Lord's Prayer and make the sign of the cross every night. Through the years, he had never gone back on his promise.

Espinosa was not lacking in spirit; one day with more indifference than anger, he had exchanged two of three punches with a group of fellow-students who were trying to force him to take part in a university demonstration. Owing to an acquiescent nature, he was full of opinions, or habits of mind, that were questionable: Argentina mattered less to him than a fear that in other parts of the world people might think of us as Indians; he worshipped France but despised the French; he thought little of Americans but approved the fact that there were tall buildings, like theirs, in Buenos Aires; he believed the gauchos of the plains to be better riders than those of hill or mountain country. When his cousin Daniel invited him to spend the summer months out at La Colorada, he said yes at once—not because he was really fond of the country, but more out of his natural complacency and also because it was easier to say yes than to dream up reasons for saying no.

The ranch's main house was big and slightly run-down; the quarters of the foreman, whose name was Gutre, were close by. The Gutres were three: the father, an unusually uncouth son, and a daughter of uncertain paternity. They were tall, strong, and bony, and had hair that was on the reddish side and faces that showed traces of Indian blood. They were barely articulate. The foreman's wife had died years before.

There in the country, Espinosa began learning things he never knew, or even suspected—for example, that you do not gallop a horse when approaching settlements, and that you never go out riding except for some special purpose. In time, he was to come and tell the birds apart by their calls.

After a few days, Daniel had to leave for Buenos Aires to close a deal on some cattle. At most, this bit of business might take him a week. Espinosa, who was already somewhat weary of hearing about his cousin's incessant luck with women and his tireless interests in the minute details of men's fashion, preferred staying on at the ranch with his textbooks. But the heat was unbearable, and even the night brought no relief. One morning at daybreak, thunder woke him. Outside, the wind was rocking the Australian pines. Listening to the first heavy drops of rain, Espinosa thanked God. All at once, cold air rolled in. That afternoon, the Salado overflowed its banks.

The next day, looking out over the flooded fields from the gallery of the main house, Baltasar Espinosa thought that the stock metaphor comparing the pampa to the sea was not altogether false—at least, not that morning—though W. H. Hudson had remarked that the sea seems wider because we view it from a ship's deck and not from a horse or from eye level.

The rain did not let up. The Gutres, helped or hindered by Espinosa, the town dweller, rescued a good part of the livestock, but many animals were drowned. There were four roads leading to La Colorada, all of them under water. On the third day, when a leak threatened the foreman's house, Espinosa gave the Gutres a room near the tool shed, at the back of the main house. This drew them all closer; they ate together in the big dining room. Conversation turned out to be difficult. The Gutres, who knew so much about country things, were hard put to explain them. One night, Espinosa asked them if people still remembered the Indian raids from back when the frontier command was located there in Junin. They told him yes, but they would have given him the same answer to a question about the beheading of Charles I. Espinosa recalled his father's saying that almost every case of longevity that was cited in the country was really a case of bad memory or a dim notion of dates. Gauchos are apt to be ignorant of the year of their birth or of the name of the man who begot them.

In the whole house, there was apparently no other reading matter than a set of the *Farm Journal,* a handbook of veterinary medicine, a deluxe edition of the Uruguayan epic *Tabaré,* a *History of Shorthorn Cattle in Argentina,* a number of erotic or detective stories, and a recent novel called *Don Segundo Sombra.* Espinosa, trying in some way to bridge the inevitable after-dinner gap, read a couple of chapters of this novel to the Gutres, none of whom could read or write. Unfortunately, the foreman had been a cattle drover, and the doings of the hero, another cattle drover, failed to whet his interest. He said that the work was light, the drovers always traveled with a packhorse that carried everything they needed, and that, had he not been a drover, he never would have seen such far-flung places as the Laguna De Gomez, the town of Bragado, and the spread of the Nunez family in Chacabuco. There was a guitar in the kitchen; the ranch hands, before the time of the events I am describing, used to sit around in a circle. Someone would tune the instrument without ever getting around to playing it. This was known as a guitarfest.

Espinosa, who had grown a beard, began dallying in front of the mirror to study his new face, and he smiled to think how, back in Buenos Aires, he would bore his friends by telling them the story of the Salado flood. Strangely enough, he missed places he never frequented and never would: a corner of Cabrera Street on which there was a mailbox; one of the cement lions of a gateway on Jujuy Street, a few blocks from the Plaza del Once; an old barroom with a tiled floor, whose exact whereabouts he was unsure of. As for his brothers and his father, they would have already learned from Daniel he was isolated by the floodwaters.

Exploring the house, still hemmed in by the watery waste, Espinosa came across an English Bible. Among the blank pages at the end, the

Guthries—such was their original name—had left a handwritten record of their lineage. They were natives of Inverness; had reached the New World, no doubt as common laborers, in the early part of the nineteenth century; and had intermarried with Indians. The chronicle broke off sometime during the eighteen-seventies, when they no longer knew how to write. After a few generations, they had forgotten English; their Spanish, at the time Espinosa knew them, gave them trouble. They lacked any religious faith, but there survived in their blood, like faint tracks, the rigid fanaticism of the Calvinist and the superstitions of the pampa Indian. Espinosa later told them of this find, but they barely took notice.

Leafing through the volume, his fingers opened it at the beginning of the Gospel according to St. Mark. As an exercise in translation, and maybe to find out whether the Gutres understood any of it, Espinosa decided to begin reading them that text after every evening meal. It surprised him that they listened attentively, absorbed. Maybe the gold letters on the cover lent the book authority. It's still there in their blood, Espinosa thought. It also occurred to him that the generations of men, throughout recorded time, have always told and retold two stories—that of a lost ship which searches the Mediterranean seas for a dearly loved island, and that of a god who is crucified on Golgotha. Remembering his lessons in elocution from his schooldays in Ramos Mejia, Espinosa got to his feet when he came to the parables.

The Gutres took to bolting their barbecued meat and their sardines so as not to delay the Gospel. A pet lamb that the girl adorned with a small blue ribbon had injured itself on a strand of barbed wire. To stop the bleeding, the three had wanted to apply a cobweb to the wound, but Espinosa treated the animal with some pills. The gratitude that this treatment awakened in them took him aback. (Not trusting the Gutres at first, he'd hidden away in one of his books the two hundred and forty pesos he had brought with him.) Now, the owner of the place away, Espinosa took over and gave timid orders, which were immediately obeyed. The Gutres, as if lost without him, liked following him from room to room and along the gallery that ran around the house. While he read to them, he noticed that they were secretly stealing the crumbs he had dropped on the table. One evening, he caught them unawares, talking about him respectfully, in very few words.

Having finished the Gospel according to St. Mark, he wanted to read another of the three Gospels that remained, but the father asked him to repeat the one he had just read, so that they could understand it better. Espinosa felt that they were like children, to whom repetition is more pleasing than variations or novelty. That night he dreamed of the Flood; the hammer blows of the building of the Ark woke him up, and he thought that perhaps they were thunder. In fact, the rain, which had let up, had started again. The cold was bitter. The Gutres had told him that the storm had damaged the roof to the toolshed, and that they would show it to him when the beams were fixed. No longer a stranger now, he was treated by them with special attention, almost to the point of spoiling him. None of them liked coffee, but for him there was always a small cup into which they heaped sugar.

The new storm had broken out on a Tuesday. Thursday night, Espinosa was awakened by a soft knock at his door, which—just in case—he always kept locked. He got out of bed and opened it; there was the girl. In the dark, he could hardly make her out, but by her footsteps he could tell that she was barefoot, and moments later, in bed, that she must have come all the way from the other end of the house naked. She did not embrace him or speak a single word; she lay beside him trembling. It was the first time she had known a man. When she left, she did not kiss him; Espinosa realized that he didn't even know her name. For some reason that he did not want to pry into, he made up his mind that upon returning to Buenos Aires he would tell no one about what had taken place.

The next day began like the previous ones, except that the father spoke to Espinosa and asked him if Christ had let Himself be killed so as to save all other men on earth. Espinosa, who was a freethinker but who felt committed to what he had read to Gutres, answered, "Yes, to save everyone from Hell."

Gutre then asked, "What's Hell?"

"A place under the ground where souls burn and burn."

"And the Roman soldiers who hammered in the nails—were they saved, too?"

"Yes," said Espinosa, whose theology was rather dim.

All along, he was afraid that the foreman might ask him about what had gone on the night before with his daughter. After lunch, they asked him to read the last chapters over again.

Espinosa slept a long nap that afternoon. It was a light sleep, disturbed by persistent hammering and by vague premonitions. Toward evening, he got up and went out onto the gallery. He said, as if thinking aloud, "The waters have dropped. It won't be long now."

"It won't be long now," Gutre repeated, like an echo.

The three had been following him. Bowing their knees to the stone pavement, they asked his blessing. Then they mocked at him, spat on him, and shoved him toward the back part of the house. The girl wept. Espinosa understood what awaited him on the other side of the door. When they opened it, he saw a patch of sky. A bird sang out. A goldfinch, he thought. The shed was without a roof; they had pulled down the beams to make a cross.

SUMMARY:

1. Baltasar Espinosa, a young, well-spoken scholar, is invited by his cousin to vacation at La Colorada ranch, which lies in the Argentine countryside.

2. The ranch is maintained by the Gutres; a father, son and daughter. After a short time, the cousin must return to Buenos Aires on business, leaving Espinosa with the Gutres.

3. Suddenly, a thunderstorm breaks, stifling the oppressive heat. The rain does not let up, drowning cattle and submerging roads to the ranch.

4. On the third day, a leak in the roof of the foreman's house necessitates a move into the main house, where Espinosa lives.

5. As the rain continues, Espinosa finds himself entertaining the silent Gutres by reading to them. When he runs out of material, he opens the Bible

and reads to them the Gospel according to St. Mark.

6. Espinosa saves an ailing lamb belonging to the daughter with pills, earning overwhelming gratitude.

7. Espinosa tries to read other books of the Bible, but the Gutres insist he repeat the Gospel according to St. Mark. At night, Espinosa dreams of the proverbial Flood; by day, he finds himself catered to by the Gutres.

8. One day, the father asks if Christ let Himself be killed to save all other men on earth, and Espinosa answers yes. He naps, bothered by the sound of hammering. When he wakens, he notices the waters have dropped. He is ushered outside by the Gutres, who have built a cross on which to crucify him.

".... And damned if Clem Chickasaw wern't killed last week, sleeping off a drunk at Grass Range. Seems Clem had a little more rye on board than usual, but not enough to suit him. So the sumbitch goes and takes a booze joint. After smoking up the place and running everybody out he helps himself to the hooch and falls asleep. Folks said they could hear him snoring all the way out on the Honeyquim spread. Well, the booze boss gets a gun and comes back and catches Clem slumberin'. Old Clem never woke up, but he quit snoring."

From a letter by Judge Roy "Tall" Cotten to his brother.
Amarillo, Texas, 1873.

ULTIMATE JOURNEY

by Bruce Bonney

On June 6 of last year, tremendous waves born of the most violent storm ever recorded in the Atlantic journeyed thousands of miles to the Gulf of Guinea to pound the secluded beaches of West Africa with such force that the vibrations were recorded at the Lamont Geological Observatory, Columbia University, New York, as well as other scattered global recording stations. The storm lasted two days. The vibrations pulsed most strongly every 27 seconds for eight hours. Because the tidal gauges at the Lamont Observatory were not functioning at the time, the precise size of the waves is unknown; however, resident oceanographer Dr. J. Oliver remarked that, "a height beyond 40 meters is a virtual certainty."

How great were such waves as to shake an entire planet when breaking? The terrible beauty of this spectacle shall remain unknown. Fleeing far inland at the first sign of trouble, a few scattered fishermen were the only witnesses. Or were they?

The dirt road south from Campo described a curving route through mangrove swamps and towering mahogany. The tick-snap-tick of cicadas and the cries of toucans were drowned out by grinding gears and squealing brakes as the old truck slowed for ruts left by the monsoon rains. The truck lurched from the canopy of mahogany branches, plowed through the white sand, and stopped. Four young surfers hopped out and surveyed their surroundings.

An old man from Campo had told them of this place. Everywhere but here the shallow bottoms caused the surf to section out without hope of allowing a satisfying ride. The beach was flat and sandy to the south. To the north, the waves wrapped around a sand bar at the base of an extended shelf of rocks. Noting the pageant of perfect waves coursing into the beach, the four quickly unloaded their boards.

"Paradise..." said Phil.

John started to lock the truck, then realized the closest fishing waters were forty miles north; Campo and civilization was two hours back along the lonely dirt road. John left the keys in the passenger-side door and grabbed his board.

"Watch out for fins," Phil said, recalling the strings of jagged yellow shark teeth covering the walls of the old man's shack. With this in mind, they slipped into the eighty-degree water and stroked toward the lineup. Sharks or not, it felt good having paradise all to themselves.

The sun was high, the only clouds hanging low on the western horizon. The waves were crisp, four to six feet, and perfectly shaped. Richard got the first ride, paddling twice and whip-turning right to stand still as a statue, passing his hand through the thin wall.

In the afternoon, the sets suddenly jumped to ten feet. They moved outside and rode the overhead sets with skillful poise. Each man had an unforgettable ride, climbing and carving and dropping with ease as the barrels peeled off evenly from the sand bar. A lateral current flowed to the north, so slight that it seemed unimportant.

Thick green lines appeared on the horizon, and Pat yelled "Outside!" They barely managed to paddle over the lineups.

"Those were pushing fifteen feet!" Phil said excitedly.

"Can't be real," said Richard, quickly paddling out to get in the best position for the next set.

Suddenly, vicious currents began ripping at the bottom. Brown, sandy water surged to the surface, and the lateral drift changed to a powerful, threatening riptide, pulling north to the rocks. In their excitement, the surfers were oblivious to the changing conditions, and having gained what they thought to be the last break line, prepared to ride what they believed was the set of the day, or perhaps the year.

Meanwhile, John was furiously paddling straight out. Some deep, animal instinct had taken hold of his limbs and wouldn't let him stop. Phil, Pat and Richard had gathered during the lull, and looked confusedly out at John, stroking still, straight out to sea. "What's with John?" Phil asked. "He's been in big surf before."

"Spooked, I guess," Pat chuckled, straddling his board and searching the horizon for the next set.

"About what?" Richard asked. "These babies haven't lost any of their form."

John's faint cry of "Outside!" drifted across the water.

Pat glanced toward the beach to discover the grim truth: "The rocks! We're on the rocks!" Now they were without the luxury of loosing their boards or the alternative of proning into the beach. "I don't like this," Pat said in a tight voice.

"Better paddle over to the sandy section and go in," advised Richard.

"Yeah, like right now," Phil agreed, dropping to his stomach and stroking hard. The others followed, but it was no good. The lateral drift was too strong, holding them stationary when they paddled and sweeping them along when they rested. They knew of the sandy beaches to the north, but they would be on the rocks before then. They could only try to paddle straight out, hoping to gain the safe water beyond the break line. Then, John became hysterical, shouting and screaming and pointing west.

They saw what he had seen, but did not dare to believe. Lineups, virtually unlimited in number, were marching in from the Atlantic. The first waves of the set topped thirty feet, and the towering peaks of the ones behind were clearly visible.

Richard shouted, "We've got to catch a wave here and now—cut right and drive for the sandy beach past the rocks—turn in and prone to the beach. We don't go now, we're history!"

The plan seemed the only one: To overcome the riptides with the greater strength of the waves. They had ridden Waimea and Makaha—the biggest surf in the business—and were familiar with these places. But now they were dealing with strange, unpredictable waves, breaking on a bottom reformed in minutes by brute force. It was impossible to imagine an arena where man should have fewer claims and less authority. Richard, the champion, was first to try.

"Get it, Rich!" Pat yelled.

Paddling at a sharp angle to the peak, Richard pressed to his feet only after his board was nearly vertical on the face. He quickly leveled off, arcing across the great green wall. Backwash surged beneath him, but he held his balance. The backwash hit a second time, and he began swerving. He bent, grabbed the left rail of his board and pulled into the steepening wall, driving in a full crouch position. He glanced down and realized that he had cleared the rocks, but the wave suddenly opened beneath him, leaving a vertical drop. Now airborne, his board free-fell away. Pitching head-over-heels down the face, he drew a quick breath, and dove. The currents, which he had thought of defeating, now pulled him toward the rocks. Each wave found him closer and closer, and he was very, very tired. Soon, the jagged black teeth were only feet away. One more wave, and he was gone.

Pat and Phil had not seen the wipeout, and felt rallied by their friend's apparent success.

"Okay, Pat. See you on the beach!"

Phil caught a beautiful wave, leaning into a smooth right turn, captivated by the immense tunnel arching behind him. Falling victim to self-confidence and the misleading excellence of the wave, he turned into the tunnel, seemingly formed of green, polished glass. Far behind were darkness and cascading thunder. Then, the wave became erratic and, shifting speed, took on the aspect of a swift and deadly Banzai "pipe." Fear returned. He dropped for additional speed, carved a sharp bottom turn and shot out onto the unbroken shoulder. Close behind, the colossus folded and collapsed, compressing a huge volume of air that roared from the tunnel like a cannon blast, blowing Phil off his board. Blinded by spray, he cartwheeled hopelessly down the face. He could hear the bottom grinding and moaning, as tons of water and boulders were summoned into the breaking wall. Phil sensed his vertical motion as the wave drew him slowly up its face to the curling apex. A moment of weightlessness, and Phil was launched over the falls as never before. And never again.

Pat had seen Phil's board spiraling high into the air, and knew what had occurred, knew that the world had gone mad. The sky and the sea were wind-whipped and slat grey. Howling, hungry waves and boiling white water had created an inescapable nightmare. Pat's fear of the sea was now the greatest he had ever known. He felt his only chance was to paddle straight out and try to reach the calm safety far from shore, and find John if possible.

Ten minutes later, Pat found himself paddling over the biggest wave he had ever seen or imagined. He knew immediately that this wave had been the first and smallest of a second set, for he had seen the endless procession when the wave had passed beneath him. He was too far inside, with neither the time nor the strength to paddle out past the breakline, and knew that he must try the original plan or perish. He turned and hesitated, glancing over his shoulder in disbelief at the horrendous gathering of energy. Forty feet at least. How mad that he should attempt such a wave as this.

Pat held his board high on the wall, considering the bottomless drop with both terror and fascination. He turned, stroked three times, settled into a low crouch and began to race the wave. Fast, incredibly fast. His board began to vibrate as he dropped with mounting speed. The giant wave began to hiss and grind, walling up in both directions. It jumped up to fifty feet, and he was locked in. Crouching lower still, he clasped a rail, leaned into titanic wall and cried, "Hold. Please, dear God, make it hold!" Sixty feet. A curtain of spume howled off the lip far overhead. Again, Pat dropped for speed, praying to reach a point where he could straighten off and prone into the sandy beach. But he arrived at the bottom too quickly, and the nose of his board knifed underwater, the tail snapping up and catapulting him a great distance. He was unaware of his shattered arms as the riptide pulled him erect. For one eternal second, his feet touched the craggy bottom as he stood to face his executioner, towering above him so far that its summit was lost to the mist. It arched as a closing hand, and broke.

John was alone now, nearly two miles from shore. He felt relatively safe, continually taking precautions against drifting in too far. The sun had set hours before, and a pale moon hung at 9 o'clock. Once, he thought he saw the distant lights of Campo. Far inside he could hear the periodic thunder of the inside break. John could not tell if he was beyond the rocks, but it did not matter now, for he would die trying *anything* to reach the beach. However long it took, he was resigned to weather the storm and paddle in after it had passed.

His friends were gone. John knew this because they would have signaled him with the truck's lights or a fire. He was both saddened and angered that there had been no one present to see and tell of their destruction, and to think, as he thought now, of how small man really was. Man and the sea would always be unequal contestants.

Suddenly, the moon vanished. John realized that he was in the shadow of a wave. He checked and knew that he had not drifted. The wave lifted him so high he could see the raging confusion of the inside break, the white, moonblanched beaches and the dark mahogany groves behind.

Paradise...

The great wave passed beneath him, moving silently until crashing nearly two-thousand yards behind him. Cold spray drenched his back. A second wave swelled up before him, only larger and moving much faster. It took nearly a minute to paddle over, finally rolling through ten feet of foam at its threatening crest. A third and a fourth, each consecutively more powerful. A set! A set at this distance! It was then that he realized the incredible fact that these waves were just beginning to get big.

He heard a wave breaking far, far outside...

SUMMARY:

1. A violent storm rages in the Atlantic, forcing upon the shores of western Africa the largest waves ever recorded.

2. Four young surfers drive out to a remote spot on the west African shore, unaware of the storm but anxious to catch some waves.

3. They paddle out, and begin riding four- to six-foot waves. By afternoon, those waves have grown to ten feet, and the surfers are having the best rides of their lives.

4. Suddenly, the waves jump to fifteen feet, and vicious currents and riptides begin to disturb the surfers. The surfers realize they're in trouble, and search for escape routes. John begins to paddle out past the breakers, the other three decide to paddle back to shore.

5. The three find they can't make headway against the unruly surf, and realize that unless they make a desperate attempt to ride the waves in, they will be dashed upon the rocks.

6. Richard, the champion surfer, is first to try. He arcs across the big green wall, grabbing the rail of his board and fighting for balance until he is past the rocks. Then, the wave crashes on him, and he is suddenly airborne. He tries to swim to safety, but the sea dashes him against the rocks.

7. The others have not seen Richard's wipeout; Phil is the next to try. He finds himself in a pipe of green water. The pipe collapses on him, squeezing him out for a moment of weightlessness before launching him over the falls to his death.

8. Pat, who watches Phil lose it, decides to follow John and points his board out to sea. But soon he realizes he'll never get beyond the wall of 40-foot waves that are approaching. He reluctantly decides he too has to try to ride one of the monsters in to shore, and, like the others, dies in the process.

9. John thinks he has found refuge on his board about two miles from shore. The sun has set, but he sees no lights on the beach, and knows his friends have perished. Suddenly, the moon disappears behind a giant wave, and John realizes this is the first in a giant set of waves—waves that were just starting to get big.

FULL FATHOM FIVE

by William Shakespeare

Full fathom five thy father lies;
   Of his bones are coral made;
Those are pearls that were his eyes:
   Nothing of him that doth fade
But doth suffer a sea change
Into something rich and strange.
Sea-nymphs hourly call his knell:
   Ding-dong. Ding dong bell.

Ariel's Song from *The Tempest*
by William Shakespeare

UNDER THE GLASS BUBBLE

by John Long

Searching for Salathea's grave was the kind of offbeat quest that suited Jeff perfectly. Like most crack adventurers I've known, Jeff Wills and common society were barely on speaking terms. From certain angles he was twenty-eight, from others, fifty. His stormy face—his whole body, really—resembled a jagged limestone statue struck to life, and this troubled some people; nobody felt comfortable before his restless eyes. And he was a mean bastard. Literally. He'd been pawned off at birth to a string of foster parents he'd never talk about. I was probably the only person who knew this, or that his natural father hailed from Riverside, a few miles away. Or at least Jeff thought he did, though I never knew how he found that out and never pressed him about it. I did know Jeff spent years trying to find him, but never could and finally gave up. The whole business drove him away from entangling relationships and straight down the Blue Nile in East Africa and the fuming Coruh in Turkey, historical first descents that both times killed his partners and cast a thundercloud over his calling and his life. Maybe it was because I was a couple years older, or had taken Jeff on his first Class 5 river—the Frazier, in Canada—but we got on well enough and always had.

Every Wednesday afternoon throughout one summer, a dozen of us would meet at the base of Mt. Roubidoux (hardly a mountain, just a swollen knoll a couple miles square and three-hundred feet high). Just west lies the Roubidoux Wash, a scrubby grey arroyo that for ten months a year teems with poison sumac and yellow jackets; but when July comes and burns the snow off distant San Gregornio, a seasonal river, narrow and treacherous, tears through the wash at speed. During that one summer we must have paddled the twelve miles through the wash a dozen times. And every trip, to and from, we'd pass the little graveyard in Mt. Roubidoux's eastern shadow, with its rococoesque headstones and moldering statues, its little marble chambers girded by rusting chains.

One Wednesday, when the smog was like ink and the mercury pressed 90, nobody showed but Jeff and me. He'd brought a six-pack of beer, so we skipped the paddling, sat in the lee of a boulder and popped a couple. We weren't four cans into it when Jeff asked if I knew about Salathea. I laughed. Somebody was always nudging the running joke along—that legendary Swiss explorer John Salathea was buried in the cemetery below. I don't know who started the ludicrous tale, but nobody believed it. When Jeff asked me if I absolutely *knew* it was bunk, I understood what he was getting at. We were out of beer and had nothing better to do.

For half an hour we wandered around the cemetery. I'd been in other boneyards before, but mostly your Forest Lawn variety, vast, shady grounds like billion-dollar golf courses, with towering "Roman" statues and enough cut flowers to make a man with a hangnail long to die. I wouldn't call the Roubidoux Memorial Cemetery a sacrilege to the dead, but the place hadn't seen a proper trimming in years, and much of the lawn resembled a wheat field, though rockier.

Most gravesites were from the middle of the last century, when anyone with money built the departed a little shrine. On the grand and forgotten headstones we read names like Sean O'Mally and Ricardo Vinicelli, first-generation Americans whose very bones were dust. One marble headstone, under a patina of lichen, read: "Timothy Macinnis A Scotsman 1869." The place seemed to have a voice to it, but it was so muted and long-ignored that I'd never make out the words until I too was host to the dead. We needed particulars. There were only names. A strange moment. We never even looked for John Salathea's grave.

Walking back to our cars, we passed over a charred section of crab grass, and Jeff suddenly tripped on a corner of gravestone. The mower and hose never reached this part of the lot. The coarse turf had completely overtaken dozens of little stone plots which, had Jeff not tripped on one, we would never have suspected were even there. We pulled back the patch of grass and scraped the soil off the one-foot-square piece of slate Jeff had stumbled over. It read: "Dorothy Ann Reniky 1912–1932." I lingered over it, knowing it might have been fifty years since someone had noticed this woman's name.

I've never bothered tangling with impossible questions, but I could not help wondering who Dorothy Ann Reniky was, or had been, and what it meant to drop into the world, drift through 20 quick years and then fade under a shroud of crab grass. It didn't take much imagination to see my own name chiseled on that little square of stone.

We pulled the grass off a bunch of other graves as well, just to let the light play across the inscriptions. On several, there were little glass bubbles, cloudy and calcified, near the bottoms of the gravestones. Jeff took off his shirt and rubbed the raised glass of one grave, which grew more and more transparent. Begrudgingly, beneath the glass bubble, an old, very small portrait came slowly into focus. Not quick enough for Jeff, however, who spit on the glass bubble and put all of himself into the work. In moments, the glass cleared, and staring out at the world was a remarkably well-preserved photo of a boy, too young to talk, certainly, though his huge, bucolic smile spoke to us. The inscription said Miguel Domingo Santana had died in 1929, aged two. His cackle had been silent for sixty years, but now you could hear the echo.

We quickly located the rest of the gravestones that had those portraits, and we set to polishing, feeling responsible for a resurrection of a kind. We'd peeled back the grass and the years and all kinds of folk were part of the continuum again. Jeff, meanwhile, had moved to the flanks, where several newer gravestones lay bare to the sun. One had a glass bubble. Jeff started buffing it clean. Suddenly, the shirt froze in Jeff's hand and his features set like the day of judgement, his eyes riveting the small picture beneath the bubble. The inscription said Milton H. Roth had died the previous year. A little figuring told us he'd been 61. He must have died broke to get planted in that blighted patch of weeds. The photo was from when Milton Roth had been young and hale. The limestone face, the nervous eyes—Jeff might as well have been looking into a mirror.

SUMMARY:

1. My offbeat friend Jeff Wills and I, both kayakers, often head off into the shadow of Mt. Roubidoux to ride the seasonal river that washes through the area in midsummer. Jeff is a hard character, who

has lived with foster parents though his natural father is rumored to reside in nearby Riverside.

2. One day, however, we decide not to paddle the river, instead settling in with a six-pack of beer. Jeff asks if I want to help find the grave of Salathea, the legendary Swiss explorer who is rumored to be buried in the tiny Mt. Roubidoux cemetery.

3. We begin to explore the cemetery, a mean, unkempt place. There, we find graves dating back to 1869. I wonder about the people who have been buried there, with their graves untended, thinking that we're the first people who've looked at them in years.

4. As we are leaving the cemetery, we stumble upon another group of graves. These, we notice, have little glass bubbles on them. Jeff cleans one off, and finds the face of the occupant of the grave preserved beneath.

5. We clean off more glass bubbles. Suddenly, Jeff freezes. The name on the grave is Milton Roth; he'd died the year before. The face in the bubble is Jeff's face.

TO THE WORLD!!

Troubled by mudslinging in modern politics? Note the following hand-bill distributed on election day in an 1847 campaign in Oregon. Thornton won.

TO THE WORLD!!
J. QUINN THORNTON,

Having resorted to low, cowardly and dishonorable means, for the purpose of injuring my character and standing, and having refused honorable satisfaction, which I have demanded; I avail myself of this opportunity of publishing him to the world as an anvilpate, a reclaimless liar, and infamous scoundrel, a blackhearted villian, an errant coward, a worthless vagabond and an imported miscreant, a disgrace to the profession and a dishonor to his country.

James W. Nesmith
Oregon City, June, 7, 1847

"WITHOUT ANYTHING TO EAT BUT THE DEAD"

*I*irginia Reed was thirteen when her family joined the Donner-Reed party *on its doomed journey to California. Here, she describes this fabled American tragedy in a letter to her cousin. To preserve its historical significance, the letter was printed verbatim in Tony Hillerman's excellent "Best of the West" (my source). Aside from correcting misspellings and a few non-words, plus adding the barest punctuation (the original has none), what follows is precisely what Virginia Reed wrote in 1846. There is a very garbled passage at the end of the letter that I tried to sort out dozens of ways, but none of my versions felt right. So I've left it alone, leaving the reader to unravel the only riddle of this remarkable document.*

May the 16 1847
My Dear Cousin

I take this opportunity to write to you to let you know that we are all well at present and hope this letter may find you well too. My dear cousin I am going to write to you about our troubles getting to California. We had good luck till we came to Big Sandy. There we lost our best yoke of oxen. We sold some of our provisions and bought a yoke of cows and oxen and they persuaded us to take the Hastings cut over the salt plain. They said it saved three-hundred miles. We went that road and we had to go through a long drive of forty miles without water or grass. Hastings said it was forty but I think it was eighty miles. We traveled a day and night and another day and at noon Pa went on to see if he could find water. He had not been gone long till some of the oxen gave out and we had to leave the wagons and take the oxen on to water. One of the men stayed with us and others went on with the cattle to water. Pa was coming back to us with water and met the men and they was about ten miles from water. Pa said they'd get to water that night, and the next day to bring the cattle back to the wagons and bring some water. Pa got to us about noon. The man that was with us took the horse and went on to water. We waited there. Thought they would come. We waited till night and we thought we start and walk to Mr. Donner's wagon that night. We took what little water we had and started. Pa carried Thomas and all the rest of us walk. We got to Donner and they were all asleep so we laid down on the ground. We spread one shawl down. We laid down on it and spread another over us and then put the dogs on top. It was the coldest night you most ever saw. The wind blew and if it hadn't been for the dogs we would have frozen. As soon as it was light we went to Mrs. Donners. She said we could not walk to the water and if we stayed we could ride in the wagons to the spring, so Pa went on to the water to see why they did not bring the cattle. When he got there there was but one ox and cow there. None of the rest had got to water. Mr. Donner come out that night with his cattle and brought his wagons and all of us in. We stayed there a week and hunted for our cattle and could not find them so some of the company took theirs and went out and brought in one wagon and cached the other two and a great many things, all but what we could put in one wagon. We had to divide our possessions out to them to get them to carry them. We got three yoke with our ox and our cow. So we went on that way for awhile and got out of provisions and Pa had to go on to California for provisions. We could not get along that way. In two or three days after Pa left we had to cache our wagon and take Mr. Graves wagon and cache some more of our things. Well we went on that way awhile and then we had to get Mr. Eddies wagon. We went on that way awhile and then we had to cache all our clothes except a change or two and put them in Mr. Brins wagon and Thomas and James rode the two horses and the rest of us had to walk. We went on that way awhile and we come to another long drive of forty miles and then we went with Mr. Donner.

We had to walk all the time we was a walking up the Truckee River. We met that and two Indians we had sent out for provisions to Sutter Fort. They had met Pa, not far from Sutter Fort. He looked very bad. He had not ate but three times in seven days and the days without anything his horse was not able to carry him. They gave him a horse and he went on so we cached all but what we could pack on one mule and we started. Martha and James rode behind the two Indians. It was a raining then in the valleys and snowing in the mountains so we went on that way three or four days till we come to the big mountain or the California mountain. The snow then was about three feet deep. There was some wagons there. They said they had attempted to cross but could not. Well we thought we would try it so we started and they started again with their wagons. The snow was then way to the mule's side. The farther we went up the deeper the snow got so the wagons could not go so they packed their oxen and started with us carrying a child apiece and driving the oxen in snow up to their waist. The mule Martha and the Indian was on was the best one so they went and broke the road. And that Indian was the pilot so we went on that way two miles and the mules kept falling down in the snow head foremost and the Indian said he could not find the road. We stopped and let the Indian and man go on to hunt the road. They went on and found the road to the top of the mountain and came back and said they thought we could get over if it did not snow anymore. Well the women were all so tired carrying three children that they could not go over that night so we made a fire and got something to eat and Ma spread down a buffalo robe and we all laid down on it and spread something over us and Ma sit up by the fire and it snowed one foot on top of the bed so we got up in the morning and the snow was so deep we could not go over and we had to go back to the cabin and build more cabins and stay there all winter without Pa. We had not the first thing to eat. Ma made some arrangements for some cattle giving two for one in California. We seldom thought of bread for we had not had any since [words illegible] and the cattle was so poor they could not hardly get up when they laid down. We stopped there the 4th of November and stayed till March and what we had to eat I can't hardly tell you and we had that man and Indians to feed. Well they started over on foot and had to come back so they made snowshoes and started again and it come on a storm and they had to come back. It would snow ten days before it would stop. They waited till it stopped and started again. I was a going with them and I took sick and could not go. There was 15 started and 7 got through, 5 women and 2 men. It come a storm and they lost the road and got out of provisions and the ones that got through had to eat them that died. Not long after they started we got out of provisions and had to put Martha at one cabin, James at another, Thomas at another. And Ma and Eliza and Milt Eliot and I dried up what little meat we had and started to see if we could get across and had to leave the children. Oh Mary you may think that hard to leave them with strangers and did not know whether we would see them again or not. We could hardly get away from them but we told them we would bring them bread and then they was willing to stay. We went and was five days out in the mountains. Ellie give out and had to go back. We went on a day longer. We had to lay bye a day and make snowshoes and we went on awhile and could not find the road and we had to turn back. I could get on very well while I thought we were getting along but as soon as we had to turn back I could hardly get along but we got to the cabins that night. I froze one of my feet very bad and that very night was the worst storm we had that winter and if we had not come back that night we would never got back. We had nothing to eat but ox hides. Oh Mary I would cry and wish I had what you all wasted. Ellie had to go to Mr. Graves cabin and we stayed at Mr. Breen. They had meat all the time and we had to kill little Cash the dog and eat him. We ate his head and feet and hide and everything about him. Oh my dear cousin you don't know what trouble is. Many a time we had the last thing on a cooking and did not know where the next would come from but there was always someway provided.

There was 15 in the cabin we was in and half of us had to lay a bed all the time. There was ten starved to death. There we was hardly able to walk. We lived on little Cash a week and after Mr. Breen would cook his meat we would take the bones and boil them 3 or 4 days at a time. Ma went down to the other cabin and got half a hide carried it in snow up to her waist.

It snowed and would cover the cabin so we could not get out for 2 or 3 days. We would have to cut pieces of the logs inside to make a fire with. I could not eat the hides and had not eat anything 3 days. Pa started out [back] to us with provisions and then come a storm and he could not go. He cache his provision and went back on the other side of the bay to get company of men but the San Joaquin got so high he could not cross. Well they made up a company at Sutter Fort and sent out. We had not ate anything for 3 days and we had only half a hide and we was out on top of the cabin and we seen them coming.

Oh my dear cousin you don't know how glad I was, we run and meet them. One of them we knew. We had traveled with them [him] on the road. They stayed there three days so they could recruit a little so we could go. There was 20 started. All of us started and went a piece and Martha and Thomas give out so the men had to take them back. Ma and Eliza, James and I come on and oh Mary that was the hardest thing yet, to come on and leave them there. Did not know but what they would starve to death. Martha said well Ma if you don't see me again do the best you can. The men said they could hardly stand it. It made them all cry but they said it was better for all of us to go on for if we was to go back we would eat that much more from them. They give them a little meat and flour and took them back and we come on. We went over a great high mountain as straight as stair steps in snow up to our knees. Little James walk the whole way over all the mountain in snow up to his waist. He said every step he took he was getting nearer Pa and something to eat. But the bears took the provision the men had cached and we had but very little to eat. When we had traveled 5 days we met Pa with 13 men going to the cabins. Oh Mary you do not know how glad we was to see him. We had not seen him for months. We thought we would never see him again. He heard we was coming and he made some sweet cakes to give us. He said he would see Martha and Thomas the next day. He went in 2 days what took us 5. Some of the company was eating from them that died but Thomas and Martha had not ate any. Pa and the men started with 12 people. Hiram O. Miller carried Thomas and Pa carried Martha and they were caught in [illegible word] and they had to stop 2 days. It stormed so they could not go and the bears took their provision and they were 4 days without anything. Pa and Hiram and all the men and one of Donner boys started. Pa a carrying Martha, Hiram carrying Thomas and the snow was up to their waist and it a snowing so they could hardly see the way. They wrapped the children up and never took them out for 4 days and they had nothing to eat in all that time. Thomas asked for something to eat once. Those that they brought from the cabins some of them was not able to come on and some would not come. There was 3 died and the rest eat them. They was 10 days without anything to eat but the dead. Pa brought Tom and Paddy on to where we was. None of the men was able to go. Their feet was froze very bad so they was another company went and brought them all in but five. Men went out after them and was caught in a storm and had to come back. There was another company gone there. Half got through that was stopped there [?] sent to their relief. There was but [?] families got that all of them got [?] we was one.

Oh Mary I have not wrote you half the trouble we have but I have wrote you enough to let you know that you don't know what trouble is. But thank the good God that we all got through and the only family that did not eat human flesh. We have left everything but I don't care for that. We have got through but don't let this letter dishearten anybody and never take no cut-offs and hurry along as fast as you can.

SUMMARY:

1. Virginia Reed was thirteen years old when she and her family set off across the American West to California with the infamous Donner-Reed party.

2. She sets down the story of the troubles the group had in a letter to her cousin.

3. She describes taking the Hastings cut over the salt plain, traveling forty miles without water or grass for the oxen. The group encounters all kinds of problems finding water as they progress, losing cattle and abandoning wagons along the way.

4. Virginia's Pa leaves the group to go to California and make preparations. Meanwhile, Virginia, her mother and brothers and sisters follow the Truckee River into the Sierra Nevada. The snow, they find, is about three feet deep.

5. They set out across the mountains anyway, with Indians helping to guide the way. The snow gets deeper and deeper the farther they go. Finally, snow blocks the road over the mountains, and the group builds some cabins in which to pass the winter.

6. They have little or nothing to eat, and eventually have to send brothers and sisters to other cabins where there is hope of food.

7. Groups would try to make it over the mountains, only to be forced back by snow, which sometimes would fall for ten days in a row. Finally, Virginia, her mother, sister and another man set out across the mountains themselves. They traveled for five days, only to be turned back by the snow. When they return to cabins, it begins to snow again — the worst snow ever.

8. Finally, Virginia and her family have to eat their dog, then there is nothing left. Ten people starve to death; the rest are hardly able to walk. The survivors boil hides and bones for days to eat.

9. Finally, a group of men sent by Virginia's Pa from Sutter Fort make it to the camp. They rest for three days, then 20 pioneers set forth, including Virginia, back over the mountains.

10. After five days, they meet Virginia's Pa, who is going back to the cabins to get the rest of the family and the others.

11. The two Reeds who had remained watched the others eat some of those who had died, but Martha and Thomas did not. Pa and another man begin to carry the two children out, but were trapped by snow for four days with no food. Eventually, they made it through.

12. Those who remained at the cabins fed off those who died. Virginia thanks God they made it through and didn't have to eat those who had died.

Just about any cowboy who endured a season in a line shack had his stories about the weather.

"Cold!" exclaimed a cowpuncher. "Why, it got so dern cold one winter the flame in our candle froze stiff. Had to wait till it thawed before we could blow her out. Then it got so hot that the corn we had for the stock started popping. My horse thought the popcorn was snow and darn near froze to death."

When the first plumbing was installed on the old ranches, the outdoor spikets were always leaking, and in winter would produce impressive icycles. There's the story of the bronc from the Circle Q ranch down in San Antone who left the spiket on before a freeze. By the time he rememberd and turned it off, a tube of ice stretched all the way to old Mexico. "Them Mexicans has never seen no ice before," the old bronc said, "and they's thought it were a snake. Tried to catch it and got frostbite."

And wind? Ranchers around Del Rio, Texas, recall a wind ". . . .so strong from the west the sun was three hours late going down." That same day a citizen claimed he witnessed a hen setting against the wind lay the same egg five times.

From Stan Hoig, *Humor of the American Cowboy*

THE ADVENTURES OF SIDI-NOUMAN

from The Arabian Nights Entertainment

The Caliph Haroun-al-Raschid and his grand-vizier, Giafar, passed through a secret door and out into the open country. Here they turned towards the Euphrates, and crossing the river in a small boat, walked through that part of town which lay along the further bank, without seeing anything to call for their interference. Much pleased with the peace and good order of the city, the Caliph and his vizier made their way through a square, and came upon a crowd watching a handsome, well-dressed youth who was urging a horse at full speed round the open space, spurring and whipping the beast so cruelly that the animal was covered with foam and blood. The Caliph, astonished at this proceeding, stopped to inquire of bystanders why the youth tortured and tormented the mare in such ways, but he could learn naught save that every day at the same hour the same thing took place. Exceedingly vexed, the Caliph passed on, instructing the vizier to command the horseman to appear before him the following day.

The next eventide, after evening prayer, the Caliph entered the hall, followed shortly by the vizier who brought with him the young man, called Sidi-Nouman, who had ill-treated his horse.

"Sidi-Nouman," observed the Caliph, "I have seen horses broken all my life long, and have even broken them myself, but I have never seen a man ply both whip and shovel-iron so barbarously as by you yesterday. Still, you have not the air of a cruel man, and I would gladly believe that you did not act in this way without some reason. As I am told that it was not the first time, and indeed that every day you are to be seen flogging and spurring your horse around the square, I wish to come to the bottom of the matter. But tell me the whole truth, and conceal nothing."

Sidi-Nouman changed color as he heard these words, and his manner grew confused; but he saw plainly that there was no help for it. So

46

he prostrated himself before the throne of the Caliph and said, "Oh, Commander of the Faithful, I am by no means perfect, but I am not naturally cruel, neither do I take pleasure in breaking the law. I admit that I lashed and gored my horse with all my might, yet I have not chastised it without reason, and I trust that I shall be judged more worthy of pity than punishment.

"I will not trouble to describe my birth; it is not of sufficient distinction to deserve your Highness' attention. My ancestors were careful people, and I inherited dinars enough to enable me to live comfortably, though without show. Having therefore a modest fortune, the only thing wanting to my happiness was a wife who could return my affection, but Allah Almighty willed otherwise, for on the very day after my marriage, my bride began to try my patience in every way that was most hard to bear.

"Now, seeing that the customs of our land oblige us to marry without ever beholding the person with whom we are to pass our lives, a man has of course no right to complain as long as his wife is not absolutely repulsive or positively deformed. The first time I saw my wife unveiled, when she had been brought to my house with the usual ceremonies, I was enchanted to find that I had not been deceived in regard to the account that had been given me of her beauty. I began married life in high spirits, and the best hopes of happiness.

"The following day a grand dinner was served to us, but as my wife did not appear, I ordered a servant to call her. Still she did not come, and I waited impatiently for some time. At last she entered the room, and we took our places at the table, and plates of rice were set before us.

"I ate mine, as was natural, with a spoon, but great was my surprise to notice that my wife, instead of doing the same, drew from her pocket a little case, from which she selected a long pin, and by the help of this pin conveyed her rice grain by grain to her mouth.

"'Amina', I exclaimed in astonishment, 'Is that the way you eat rice at home? And did you do it because your appetite was so small, or did you wish to count the grains so that you might never eat more than a certain number? If it was from economy, and you are anxious to teach me not to be wasteful, you have no cause for alarm. Our fortune is large enough for all our needs, therefore, dear Amina, do not seek to check yourself, but eat as much as you desire, as I do!'

47

"In reply to my words, I expected a cheerful answer; yet Amina said nothing at all, rather continued to pick her rice as before, only at longer and longer intervals. And, instead of trying the other dishes, all she did was put every now and then a crumb of bread into her mouth, and that would not have made a meal for a sparrow.

"I felt provoked by her obstinacy, but to excuse her to myself as far as I could, I suggested that perhaps she had never been used to eat in the company of men, and that her family might have taught her that she ought to behave discreetly in the presence of her husband. Likewise that she might either have dined already, or intend to do so in her own apartments. So I took no further notice, and when I had finished I left the room, secretly much vexed at her strange conduct.

"The same thing occurred at supper, and all through the next week, whenever we ate together. It was quite clear that no woman could live upon two or three bread crumbs and a few grains of rice, and I resolved to find out how and when she got food. I pretended not to pay attention to anything she did, in the hope that little by little she would get accustomed to me, and become more friendly; but I soon saw that my expectations were quite vain.

"One night I was lying with my eyes closed, and to all appearance sound asleep, when Amina rose softly, and silently dressed herself. I could not imagine what she was going to do, and as my curiosity was great, I resolved to follow her after she stole quietly from the room.

"The instant she had let the curtain fall behind her, I flung a garment on my shoulders, and a pair of slippers on my feet. Looking from a lattice which opened into the court, I saw her stealthily pass through a street door, which she carefully left open.

"It was bright moonlight, so I easily managed to keep her in sight, till she entered a cemetery not far from the house. There I hid myself under a shadow of the wall, and crouched down cautiously; and hardly was I concealed when I saw my wife approaching in company with a ghoul—one of those demons which, as your Highness is aware, wander about the country making their lairs in deserted buildings and springing out upon unwary travelers on whose flesh they dine. If no live being goes their way, then they betake themselves to the cemeteries, and sup upon the dead.

"I was struck dumb with horror on seeing my wife with this hideous female ghoul. They began to dig up a corpse which had been buried that day, and presently sat down on the edge of the grave to enjoy their frightful repast, talking cheerfully all the while, though I was too far off to hear what they said. When they had finished, they threw back the body into the grave, and heaped back the earth upon it. I made no effort to disturb them, and returned quickly to the house, where I took care to leave the door open, as I had previously found it. Then I got back into bed, and pretended to sleep soundly.

"A short time after Amina entered as quietly as she had gone out. She undressed and stole into bed, congratulating herself apparently on the cleverness with which she had managed her expedition.

"As may be guessed, after such a scene it was long before I could close my eyes, and at the first sound which called the faithful to prayer, I put on my clothes and went to the mosque. But even prayer did not restore my troubled spirit, and I could not face my wife until I had made up my mind what future course I should pursue. I therefore spent the morning roaming about from one garden to another, turning over various plans for compelling my wife to give up her horrible ways. I thought of using violence to make her submit, but had an instinct that gentle means had the best chance of success; so a little soothed, I turned towards home, which I reached about the hour of dinner.

"As soon as I appeared, Amina ordered dinner to be served, and we sat down together. As usual, she persisted in only picking a few grains of rice.

"'Amina,' I said as quietly as possible, 'You must have guessed the surprise I felt, when the day after our marriage you declined to eat anything but a few morsels of rice, and altogether in such a manner that most husbands would have been sorely vexed. However I had patience with you, and only tried to tempt your appetite by the choicest dishes I could invent, but all to no purpose. Still, Amina, it seems to me that there be some among them as sweet to the taste as the flesh of a corpse?'

"I had no sooner uttered these words than Amina, who instantly understood that I had followed her to the graveyard, was seized with a passion beyond any that I have ever witnessed. Her face became purple, her eyes looked as if they would start from her head, and she positively foamed with rage.

"I watched her with terror as she seized a vessel of water that stood at hand, and plunging her hand in it, murmured some words I failed to catch. Then, sprinkling it on my face, she cried madly:

"'Wretch, receive the reward of your prying, and become a dog.'

"The words were not out of her mouth when, without feeling conscious that any change was passing over me, I suddenly knew that I had ceased to be a man. In the greatness of shock and surprise—for I had no idea that Amina was a magician—I never dreamed of running away, and stood rooted to the spot, while Amina grasped a stick and commenced brutally flogging me. Indeed her blows were so heavy, that I only wonder they did not kill me at once. However they succeeded in rousing me from my stupor, and I dashed into the courtyard, followed closely by Amina, who made frantic dives at me, which I was not quick enough to dodge. At last she got tired of pursuing me, or else a new trick entered into her head, which would give me speedy and painful death; she opened the gate leading into the street, intending to crush me as I passed through. Dog though I was, I saw through her design, and stung into presence of mind by the greatness of the danger, I timed my movements so that I contrived to rush through, and only the tip of my tail received a squeeze as she banged the gate.

"I was safe but my tail hurt me horribly, and I yelped and howled so loud all along the streets that the other dogs came and attacked me, which made matters no better. In order to avoid them, I took refuge in a baker's shop, which seemed to have a gay and merry man for a master. At that moment he was having his breakfast, and though I gave no signs of hunger, he at once threw me a piece of bread. Before gobbling it up, as dogs are want to do, I bowed my head and wagged my tail, in token of thanks, and he understood and smiled pleasantly. I really did not want the bread at all, but felt it would be ungracious to refuse, so I ate it slowly, in order that he might see that I only did it out of politeness. He understood this also, and seemed quite willing to let me stay in his shop, so I sat down, with my face to the door, to show that I only asked his protection. This he gave me, and indeed encouraged me to come into the house itself, giving me a corner where I might sleep, without being in anybody's way.

"The kindness heaped on me by this excellent man was far greater than I could ever have expected. He was always affectionate in his manner of treating me, and I shared his breakfast, dinner and supper, while, on my side, I gave him all the gratitude and attachment to which he had right.

"I sat with my eyes fixed on him, and he never left the house without having me at his heels; and if it ever happened that when he was preparing to go out I was asleep, and did not notice, he would call, 'Rufus, Rufus,' for that was the name he gave me.

"Some weeks passed in this way, when one day a woman came to buy bread. In paying for it, she laid down several pieces of money, one of which was bad. The baker perceived this, and declined to take it, demanding another in its place. The woman, for her part, refused to take it back, declaring it was perfectly good, but the baker would have nothing to do with it. 'It is really such a bad imitation,' he exclaimed at last, 'that even my dog would not be taken in. Here Rufus! Rufus!' and hearing his voice, I jumped to the counter. The baker threw down the money before me, and said, 'Find out if there is a bad coin.' I looked at each turn, and then laid my paw on the false one, glancing at the same time at my master, so as to point it out.

"The baker, who had of course been only in joke, was exceedingly surprised at my cleverness, and the woman, who was at last convinced that the man spoke the truth, produced another piece of money in its place. When she had gone, my master was so pleased that he told all the neighbors what I had done, and made a great deal more of it than there really was.

"The neighbors, very naturally, declined to believe his story, and tried me several times with all the bad money they could collect together, but I never failed to stand the test triumphantly.

"One day a woman, who had not been in the shop before, came to ask for bread, like the rest. As usual, I was lying on the counter, and she threw down six coins before me, one of which was false. I detected it at once, and put my paw on it, looking as I did so at the woman. 'Yes,' she said, nodding her head. 'You are quite right, that is the one.' She stood gazing at me attentively for some time, then paid for the bread, making a sign for me to follow her secretly.

"Now my thoughts were always running on some means of shaking the spell laid on me, and noticing the way in which this woman had looked at me, the idea entered my head that perhaps she might have guessed what had happened, and in this way I was not deceived. However I let her go on a little way, and merely stood at the door watching her. She turned, and seeing that I was quite still, she again beckoned me.

"The baker all this while was busy with his oven, and had forgotten all about me, so I stole out softly, and ran after the woman.

"When we came to her house, which was some distance off, she opened the door and then said to me, 'Come in, come in; you will never be sorry that you followed me.' When I entered she fastened the door, and took me into a large room where a beautiful girl was working at a piece of embroidery. 'My daughter,' exclaimed my guide, 'I have brought you the famous dog belonging to the baker which can tell good money from bad. You know that when I first heard of him, I was sure he must really be a man, changed into a dog by magic. Today I went to the baker's, to prove for myself the truth of the story, and persuaded the dog to follow me here. Now what do you say?'

'You are right, mother,' replied the girl, and rising she dipped her hand into a vessel of water. Then sprinkling it over me, she said, 'If you were born dog, remain dog; but if you were born man, by virtue of this water resume your proper form.' In one moment, the spell was broken. The dog's shape vanished as if it had never been, and it was a man who stood before her.

"Overcome with gratitude at my deliverance, I flung myself at her feet, and kissed the hem of her garment. 'How can I thank you for your goodness towards a stranger, and for what you have done? Henceforth, I am your slave. Deal with me as you will.'

"Then, in order to explain how I came to be changed into a dog, I told her my whole story, and finished with rendering the mother the thanks due to her for the happiness she had brought me.

"'Sidi-Nouman,' returned the daughter, 'say no more about the obligation you are under to us. The knowledge that we have been of service to you is ample payment. Let us speak of Amina, your wife, with whom I was acquainted before her marriage. I was aware that she was a magician, and she knew too that I had studied the same art, under the same mistress. We met often going to the same baths, but we did not like each other, and never sought to become friends. As to what concerns you, it is not enough to have broken your spell, she must be punished for her wickedness. Remain for a moment with my mother, I beg,' she added hastily, 'I will return shortly.'

"Left alone with the mother, I again expressed the gratitude I felt, to her as well to her daughter.

"'My daughter,' she answered, 'is, as you see, as accomplished a magician as Amina herself, but you would be astonished at the amount of good she does by her knowledge. That is why I have never interfered, otherwise I should have put a stop to it long ago.' As she spoke, her daughter entered with a small bottle in her hand.

"'Sidi-Nouman,' she said, 'The books I have just consulted tell me that Amina is not home at present, but she should return at any moment. I have likewise found out by their means, that she pretends before the servants great uneasiness as to your absence. She has circulated a story that, while at dinner with her, you remembered some important business that had to be done at once, and left the house without shutting the door. By this means, a dog strayed in, which she was forced to get rid of by a stick. Go home then without delay, and await Amina's return in your room. When she returns, go down to meet her, and in her surprise, she will try to run away. Then have this bottle ready, and dash the water it contains over her, saying boldly, "Receive the reward of your crimes." That is all I have to tell you.'

"Everything happened exactly as the young magician foretold. I had not been in my house many minutes before Amina returned, and as she approached I stepped in front of her, with the water in my hand. She gave one loud cry, and turned to the door, but she was too late. I had already dashed the water in her face and spoken the magic words. Amina disappeared, and in her place stood the horse you saw me beating yesterday. I marveled greatly at this transformation and seizing the mare's mane led her to the stable and secured her with a halter and lashed her with a whip till my forearm was tired. Then I resolved to ride her at speed round the square every day and inflict upon her the justest penalty.

"This, Commander of the Faithful, is my story, and may I venture to hope that, now you have heard the reason of my conduct, your Highness will not think this wicked woman too harshly treated."

SUMMARY:

1. The Caliph and his companion are traveling through the Euphrates valley when they encounter an extraordinary sight—a young man riding a horse at full speed in the square, whipping and spurring the animal ferociously.

2. The Caliph calls the young man, Sidi-Nouman, to his palace to explain this strange situation.

3. Sidi-Nouman explains that he had been well off in all ways, except for a wife. But when he married, he found his bride tried his patience. After the marriage, a grand dinner was served, but his wife, Amina, didn't come. Eventually, when she did sit with him, she ate only a grain of rice, which she skewered with a pin.

4. Sidi-Nouman was perplexed by this situation, which went on day after day, until one night, as he pretended to sleep, his wife arose softly.

5. He followed her in the bright moonlight to the cemetery, where she met with a hideous female ghoul, and the two began to feast on human flesh.

6. At the next meal, Sidi-Nouman confronted his wife, who flew into a rage and cursed him, turning him into a dog. She began to beat him, but he escaped, and began to roam the city.

7. He met a kind baker, who took him in. The baker was most impressed with his new dog's cleverness, as Sidi-Nouman was able tell false money from good.

8. One day, a woman came in, bought some bread and threw some coins on the counter to pay. Sidi Nouman picked out the false one. The woman said, "That's correct," and bade him follow her.

9. She took him to her daughter, who was, like Amina, a magician. The daughter changed him back into a man, then gave him a spell with which he could punish his evil wife.

10. Sidi-Nouman returned to his home, where he met his wife and cast the other magician's spell on her—she was transformed into the horse, which her husband justly punished in the manner witnessed by the Caliph.

he yarns and tall tales of the Wisconsin and Minnesota lumber camps include some singular creatures:

There is the *Hidebehind*, which is always hiding behind something. No matter how many times or whichever way a man turns, it is always behind him, that's why nobody has been able to describe it, even though it is credited with having killed and devoured many lumberjacks.

Among the fish of this region we find the *Upland Trout*. They nest in trees and are good fliers but are scared of water.

There's another fish, the *Goofang*, that swims backward to keep water out of its eyes. It's described as "about the same size of a sunfish, only much bigger."

We shouldn't forget the *Goofus Bird* that builds its nest upside down and flies backward, not caring where it's going, only where it's been.

And finally there's the *Gillgaloo*, which nested on the slopes of Paul Bunyan's famed Pyramid Forty, laying square eggs to keep them from rolling down the steep incline and breaking. These eggs were coveted by lumberjacks, who hard-boiled them and used them as dice.

From Jorge Luis Borges' *The Book of Imaginary Beings*

THE TELL-TALE HEART

by Edgar Allan Poe

True! Nervous—very, very dreadfully nervous I had been and am; but why will you say that I am mad? The disease had sharpened my senses, not destroyed, not dulled them. Above all was the sense of hearing acute. I heard all things in the heaven and in the earth. I heard many things in hell. How, then, am I mad? Hearken and observe how healthily, how calmly I can tell you the whole story.

It is impossible to say how first the idea entered my brain, but once conceived, it haunted me day and night. Object there was none. Passion there was none. I loved the old man. He had never wronged me. He had never given me insult. For his gold I had no desire. I think it was his eye! Yes, it was this! One of his eyes resembled that of a vulture, a pale blue eye, with a film over it. Whenever it fell upon me, my blood ran cold; and so by degrees, very gradually, I made up my mind to take the life of the old man, and thus rid myself of the eye for ever.

Now this is the point. You fancy me mad. Madmen know nothing. But you should have seen me. You should have seen how wisely I proceeded—with what caution—with what foresight—with what dissimulation I went to work! I was never kinder to the old man than during the whole week before I killed him. And every night, about midnight, I turned the latch of his door and opened it—oh, so gently! And then, when I had made an opening sufficient for my head, I put in a dark lantern, all closed, closed, so that no light shone out, and then I thrust in my head. Oh, you would have laughed to see how cunningly I thrust it in! I moved it slowly—very, very slowly, so that I might not disturb the old man's sleep. It took me an hour to place my whole head within the opening so far that I could see him as he lay upon his bed. Ha! Would a madman have been so wise as this? And then, when my head was well in the room, I undid the lantern cautiously—oh, so cautiously—cautiously (for the hinges creaked)—I undid it just so much that a single thin ray fell upon the vulture eye. And this I did for seven long nights, every night just at midnight, but I found the eye always closed; and so it was impossible to do the work; for it was not the old man who vexed me, but his Evil Eye. And every morning, when the day broke, I went boldly into the chamber, and spoke courageously to him, calling him by name in a hearty tone, and inquiring how he had passed the night. So you see he would have been a very profound old man, indeed, to suspect that every night, just at twelve, I looked in upon him while he slept.

Upon the eighth night I was more than usually cautious in opening the door. A watch's minute hand moves more quickly than did mine. Never before that night had I felt the extent of my own powers—of my sagacity. I could scarcely contain my feelings of triumph. To think that there I was, opening the door, little by little, and he not even to dream of my secret deeds or thoughts. I fairly chuckled at the idea; and perhaps he heard me, for he moved on the bed suddenly, as if startled. Now you may think that I drew back—but no. His room was as black as pitch with the thick darkness (for the shutters were close fastened, through fear of robbers), and so I knew that he could not see the opening of the door, and I kept pushing it on steadily, steadily.

I had my head in, and was about to open the lantern, when my thumb slipped upon the fastening, and the old man sprang up in the bed, crying out, "Who's there?"

I kept quite still and said nothing. For a whole hour I did not move a muscle, and in the meantime I did not hear him lie down. He was still sitting up in the bed listening, just as I had done, night after night, hearkening to the death watches in the wall.

Presently I heard a slight groan, and I knew it was the groan of mortal terror. It was not a groan of pain or of grief—oh, no!—it was the low stifled sound that arises from the bottom of the soul when overcharged with awe. I knew the sound well. Many a night, just at midnight, when all the world slept, it has welled up from my own bosom, deepening, with its dreadful echo, the terrors that distracted me. I say I knew it well. I knew what the old man felt, and pitied him, although I chuckled at heart. I knew that he had been lying awake ever since the first slight noise, when he had turned in the bed. His fears had been ever since growing upon him. He had been trying to fancy them causeless, but could not. He had been saying to himself, "It is nothing but the wind in the chimney, it is only a mouse crossing the floor," or "It is merely a cricket which has made a single chirp." Yes, he has been trying to comfort himself with these suppositions; but he had found all in vain. All in vain, because Death, in approaching him, had stalked with his black shadow before him, and enveloped the victim. And it was the mournful influence of the unperceived shadow that caused him to feel—although he neither saw nor heard—to feel the presence of my head within the room.

When I had waited a long time, very patiently, without hearing him lie down, I resolved to open a little—a very, very little crevice in the lantern. So—opened it—you cannot imagine how stealthily, stealthily, until at length, a single dim ray, like the thread of the spider, shot from out the crevice and full upon the vulture eye.

It was open—wide, wide open—and I grew furious as I gazed upon it. I saw it with perfect distinctness, all a dull blue, with a hideous veil over it that chilled the very marrow in my bones; but I could see nothing else of the old man's face or person for I had directed the ray as if by instinct, precisely upon the damned spot.

And now have I not told you that what you mistake for madness is but over-acuteness of the senses? Now, I say, there came to my ears a low, dull, quick sound, such as a watch makes when enveloped in cotton. I knew that sound well too. It was the beating of the old man's heart. It increased my fury, as the beating of a drum stimulates the soldier into courage.

But even yet I refrained and kept still. I scarcely breathed. I held the lantern motionless. I tried as steadily as I could to maintain the ray upon the eye. Meantime the hellish tattoo of the heart increased. It grew quicker and quicker, and louder and louder every instant. The old man's terror must have been extreme! It grew louder, I say, louder every moment! Do you mark me well? I have told you that I am nervous; so I am. And now at the dead hour of the night, amid the dreadful silence of that old house, so strange a noise as this excited me to uncontrollable terror. Yet, for some minutes longer I refrained and stood still. But the beating grew louder, louder! I thought the heart must burst. And now a new anxiety seized me—the sound would be heard by a neighbor! The old man's hour had come! With a loud yell, I threw open the lantern and leaped into the room. He shrieked once. Once only. In an instant I dragged him to the floor, and pulled the heavy bed over him. I then smiled gaily, to find the deed so far done. But, for many minutes, the heart beat on with a muffled sound. This, however, did not vex me; it would not be heard through the wall. At length it ceased. The old man was dead. I removed the bed and examined the corpse. Yes, he was stone, stone dead. I placed my hand upon the heart and held it there many minutes. There was no pulsation. He was stone dead. His eye would trouble me no more.

If still you think me mad, you will think so no longer when I describe the wise precautions I took for the concealment of the body. The night waned, and I worked hastily, but in silence. First of all I dismembered the corpse. I cut off the head and the arms and the legs.

I then took up three planks from the flooring of the chamber, and deposited all between the scantlings. I then replaced the boards so cleverly, so cunningly, that no human eye—not even his—could have detected any thing wrong. There was nothing to wash out—no stain of any kind—no blood-spot whatever. I had been too wary for that. A tub had caught all, ha! ha!

When I had made an end of these labors, it was four o'clock, still dark as midnight. As the bell sounded the hour, there came a knocking at the street door. I went down to open it with a light heart, for what had I now to fear? There entered three men, who introduced themselves, with perfect suavity, as officers of the police. A shriek had been heard by a neighbor during the night; suspicion of foul play had been aroused; information had been lodged at the police office, and they (the officers) had been deputed to search the premises.

I smiled, for what had I to fear? I bade the gentlemen welcome. The shriek, I said, was my own in a dream. The old man, I mentioned, was absent in the country. I took my visitors all over the house. I bade them search—search well. I led them, at length, to his chamber. I showed them his treasures, secure, undisturbed. In the enthusiasm of my confidence, I brought chairs into the room, and desired them here to rest from their fatigues, while I myself, in the wild audacity of my perfect triumph, placed my own seat upon the very spot beneath which reposed the corpse of the victim.

The officers were satisfied. My manner had convinced them. I was singularly at ease. They sat, and while I answered cheerily, they chatted familiar things. But, ere long, I felt myself getting pale and wished them gone. My head ached, and I fancied a ringing in my ears; but still they sat and still chatted. The ringing became more distinct; it continued and became more distinct; I talked more freely to get rid of the feeling; but it continued and gained definitiveness until, at length, I found that the noise was not within my ears.

No doubt I now grew very pale, but I talked more fluently, and with a heightened voice. Yet the sound increased, and what could I do? It was a low, dull, quick sound—much such a sound as a watch makes when enveloped in cotton. I gasped for breath, and yet the officers heard it not. I talked more quickly, more vehemently; but the noise steadily increased. I arose and argued about trifles, in a high key and with violent gesticulations, but the noise steadily increased. Why would they not be gone? I paced the floor to and fro with heavy strides, as if excited to fury by the observation of the men—but the noise steadily increased. Oh God! what could I do? I foamed. I raved. I swore! I swung the chair upon which I had been sitting, and grated it upon the boards, but the noise arose over all and continually increased. It grew louder— louder—louder! And still the men chatted pleasantly, and smiled. Was it possible they heard not? Almighty God! No, no! They heard! They suspected! They knew! They were making a mockery of my horror! This I thought, and this I think. But any thing was better than this agony! Any thing was more tolerable than this derision! I could bear those hypocritical smiles no longer! I felt that I must scream or die! And now— again!—hark! louder! louder! louder! louder!

"Villains!" I shrieked, "dissemble no more! I admit the deed! Tear up the planks! Here, here!—it is the beating of his hideous heart!"

SUMMARY:

1. I am quite nervous, but I must tell you my story.
2. I lived alone with an old man, who was very kind and whom I loved, but for one of his eyes, which was a pale blue and resembled that of a vulture. It made my blood run cold, and I resolved to kill the old man to rid myself of this eye.
3. For seven nights, I entered his room very slowly, very carefully, unveiling a lantern so that a single

thin ray might fall upon the vulture eye, awaiting the right opportunity.

4. On the eighth night, I slowly opened the door, but the old man awoke, crying, "Who's there?" I said nothing and stayed still, until I heard him groan with terror, then settle. When I opened the lantern, the light fell on the evil eye.

5. The sound of a muffled beating heart filled the room, and as I watched, it grew louder, until I thought a neighbor might hear, and I leapt forward, dragging the old man to the floor, where he uttered a single shriek before I smothered him with the bed.

6. To conceal the body, I cut it up and stashed it beneath the floorboards. As I finished, a knock came to the door.

7. It was three police officers, who were answering the concerns of a neighbor, who had heard the old man shriek. Fearless, I invited them in, and sat with them in the old man's chamber, telling them the old man had gone to the country.

8. As we sat, they asking questions, me answering, it began again, the sound of a muffled heartbeat.

9. As the officers chatted, it grew louder and louder, until I was sure they could hear. I became unglued, and began to rave and swear, until finally I confessed, "Tear up the planks! Here, here . . . it is the beating of his hideous heart."

Humoring the daily bread was a time-honored custom for cowboys, whether at home quarters, on the range, or off trail in some fancy city restaurant. One cowboy on a visit to town saw a sign reading:

Snack—two bits

Square meal—four bits

Bellyache—one dollar!

He entered the establishment and, when the waitress came over, ordered a dozen rotten eggs and some weak coffee. The waitress looked at him for a crazy man, but the waddie explained that he had a tapeworm and he'd be doggoned if he was going to feed it first-class chuck.

From Stan Hoig, *Humor of the American Cowboy*

THE WOMAN AT THE STORE

by Katherine Mansfield

All that day the heat was terrible. The wind blew close to the ground. It rooted among the tussock grass, slithered along the road, so that the white pumice dust swirled in our faces and settled over us like an itching dry skin. The horses stumbled along, coughing and chuffing. The pack horse was sick, with a big, open sore rubbed under the belly. Now and again she stopped short, threw back her head, looked at us as though she were going to cry, and whinnied. Hundreds of larks shrilled; the sky was slate color, and the sound of the larks reminded me of slate pencils scraping over its surface. There was nothing to be seen but wave after wave of tussock grass, patched with purple orchids and manuka bushes covered with thick spider webs.

Joe rode ahead. He wore a blue gallate shirt, corduroy trousers and riding boots. A white handkerchief, spotted with red, was knotted round his throat. Wisps of white hair straggled from under his wideawake—his moustache and eyebrows were called white. He slouched in the saddle, grunting. Not once that day had he sung:

"I don't care, for don't you see,
My wife's mother was in front of me!"

It was the first day we had been without it for a month, and now there seemed something uncanny in his silence. Jim rode beside me, white as a clown; his black eyes glittered, and he kept shooting out his tongue and moistening his lips. He was dressed in a Jagger vest, and a pair of blue duck trousers, fastened around the waist with a plaited leather belt. We had hardly spoken since dawn. At noon we had lunched off fly biscuits and apricots by the side of a swampy creek.

"My stomach feels like the crop of a hen," said Joe. "Now then, Jim, you're the bright boy of the party. Where's this 'ere store you kep' on talking about? 'Oh, yes,' you says, ' I know a fine store, with a paddock for the horses and a creek runnin' through, owned by a friend of mine who'll give yer a bottle of whiskey before 'e shakes hands with yer.' I'd like to see that place—merely as a matter of curiosity—not that I'd ever doubt yer word—as yer know very well—but. . ."

Jim laughed. "Don't forget there's a woman too, Joe, with blue eyes and yellow hair, who'll promise you something else before she shakes hands with you. Put that in your pipe and smoke it."

"The heat's making you balmy," said Joe.

He dug his knees into the horse. We shambled on. I half fell asleep, and had a sort of uneasy dream that the horses were not moving forward at all; then that I was on a rocking-horse, and my old mother was scolding me for raising such a fearful dust from the drawing-room carpet. "You've entirely worn off the pattern of the carpet," I heard her saying, and she gave the reins a tug. I snivelled and woke to find Jim leaning over me, maliciously smiling.

"What's up? Been bye-bye?"

"No!" I raised my head. "Thank the Lord we're arriving somewhere."

We were on the brow of the hill, and below us there was a whare roofed with corrugated iron. It stood in a garden, rather far back from the road, a big paddock opposite, and a creek and a clump of young willow trees. A thin line of blue smoke stood up straight from the chimney of the whare; and as I looked a woman came out, followed by a child and a sheep dog. The woman carrying what appeared to me a black stick. She made gestures at us. The horses put on a final spurt, Joe took off his wideawake, shouted, threw out his chest, and began singing, "I don't care, for don't you see. . ." The sun pushed through the pale clouds and shed a vivid light over the scene. It gleamed on the woman's yellow hair, over her flapping pinafore and the rifle in her hands. The child hid behind her, and the yellow dog, a mangy beast, scuttled back into the whare, his tail between his legs. We drew rein and dismounted.

"Hallo," screamed the woman. "I thought you was three 'awks. My kid comes runnin' in ter me. 'Mumma,' says she, 'there's three brown things comin' over the 'ill,' says she. An' I comes out smart, I can tell ye. 'They'll be 'awks.' I says to her, Oh, the 'awks about 'ere ye wouldn't believe."

The "kid" gave us the benefit of one eye from behind the woman's pinafore, then retired again.

"Where's your old man?" asked Jim.

The woman blinked rapidly, screwed up her face and said, "Away shearin'. Bin gone a month. I suppose ye not goin' to stop, are ye? There's a storm comin' up."

"You bet we are," said Joe. "So you're on your lonely, missus?"

She stood, pleating the frills of her pinafore, and glancing from one to the other of us, like a hungry bird. I smiled at the thought of how Jim had pulled Joe's leg about her. Certainly her eyes were blue, and what hair she had was yellow, but ugly. Her front teeth were knocked out, she had red pulpy hands, and she wore on her feet a pair of dirty Bluchers. Looking at her, you felt there was nothing but sticks and wires under that pinafore.

"I'll go and turn out the horses," said Jim. "Got any embrocation? Poi's rubbed herself to hell."

"'Arf a mo!" The woman stood silent a moment, her nostrils expanding as she breathed. Then she shouted violently. "I'd rather you didn't stop. You can't, and there's the end of it. I don't let out that paddock any more. You'll have to go on; I ain't got nothing!"

"Well, I'm blest!" said Joe, heavily. "Gone a bit off 'er dot," he mumbled to me. "Too much alone, you know. But turn the sympathetic tap on 'er, she'll come round all right."

But there was no need. She had come round by herself.

"Stop if ye like!" she muttered, shrugging her shoulders. "I'll give ye the embrocation if ye come along," she said to me.

"Right-o, I'll take it down to them."

We walked together up the garden path, planted on both sides with cabbages. They smelled like stale dishwater. Of flowers there were doubled poppies and sweet williams. One little patch was divided off by pawa shells—presumably it belonged to the child, for she ran from her mother and began to grub in it with a broken clothes-peg. The yellow dog lay across the doorstep, biting fleas; the woman kicked him away.

"Gar-r, get away, you beast. The place ain't tidy. I 'aven't 'ad time ter fix things today. Been ironing. Come right in."

It was a large room, the walls plastered with old pages of English periodicals. Queen Victoria's Jubilee appeared to be the most recent number. A table with an ironing board and wash tub on it, some wooden forms, a black horsehair sofa, and some broken cane chairs pushed against the walls. The mantelpiece above the stove was draped in pink paper, further ornamented with dried grasses and ferns and a colored print of Richard Seddon. There were four doors. One, judging from the smell, let into the "store," one on to the "back yard," through a third I saw the bedroom. Flies buzzed in circles round the ceiling, and treacle papers and bundles of dried clover were pinned to the window curtains.

I was alone in the room; she had gone into the store for the embrocation. I heard her stamping about and muttering to herself: "Now where did I put that bottle? It's behind the pickles. . .no, it ain't." I cleared a place on the table and sat there, swinging my legs. Down in the paddock I could hear Joe singing and the sound of hammer strokes as Jim drove in the tent pegs. It was sunset. There is no twilight in our New Zealand days, but a curious half-hour when everything appears grotesque—it frightens—as though the savage spirit of the country walked abroad and sneered at what it saw. Sitting alone in the hideous room I grew afraid. The woman next door was a long time finding that stuff. Once I thought I heard her bang her hands down on the counter, and once she half moaned, turning it into a cough and clearing her throat. I wanted to shout "Buck up!" but I kept silent.

What a life!, I thought. Imagine being here day in, day out, with that rat of a child and a mangy dog. Imagine bothering about ironing. Mad? Of course she's mad! Wonder how long she's been here. Wonder if I could get her to talk.

At that moment she poked her head round the door.

"Wot was it yer wanted?" she asked.

"Embrocation."

"Oh, yes. I got it. Was in front of the pickle jars." She handed me the bottle.

"My, you do look tired, you do! Shall I knock yer up a few scones for supper? There's some tongue in the store, too, and I'll cook yer a cabbage if you fancy it."

"Right-o." I smiled at her. "Come down to the paddock and bring the kid for tea."

She shook her head, pursing up her mouth.

"Oh no. I don't fancy it. I'll send the kid down with the things and a billy of milk. Shall I knock up a few extry scones to take with yer ter-morrow?"

"Thanks."

She came and stood by the door.

"How old is the kid?"

"Six, come next Christmas. I 'ad a bit of trouble with 'er one way an' another. I 'adn't any milk till a month after she was born and she sickened like a cow."

"She's not like you. Takes after her father?" Just as the woman had shouted her refusal at us before, she shouted at me then.

"No, she don't! She's the dead spit of me. Any fool could see that. Come on in now, Else, you stop messing in the dirt."

I met Joe climbing over the paddock fence.

"What's the old bitch got in the store?" he asked.

"Don't know, didn't look."

"Well, of all the fools. Jim's slanging you. What have you been doing all the time?"

"She couldn't find this stuff. Oh, my shakes, you are smart!"

Joe had washed, combed his wet hair in a line across his forehead, and buttoned a coat over his shirt. He grinned.

Jim snatched the embrocation from me. I went to the end of the paddock where the willows grew and bathed in the creek. The water was clear and soft as oil. Along the edges held by the grass and rushes, white foam tumbled and bubbled. I lay in the water and looked up at the trees that were still a moment, then quivered lightly, and again were still. The air smelt of rain. I forgot about the woman and the kid until I came back to the tent. Jim lay by the fire, watching the billy boil.

I asked where Joe was, and if the kid had brought our supper.

"Pooh," said Jim, rolling over and looking up at the sky. "Didn't you see how Joe had been titivating? He said to me before he went up to the whare, 'Dang it! She'll look better by night light at any rate, my buck, she's female flesh!' "

"You had Joe about her looks. Had me, too."

"No—look here. I can't make it out. It's four years since I came past this way, and I stopped here two days. The husband was a pal of mine

68

once, down the West Coast—a fine, big chap, with a voice on him like a trombone. She'd been barmaid down on the Coast, as pretty as a wax doll, she was. The coach used to come this way then once a fortnight, before they opened the railway up Napier way, and she had no end of a time! Told me once in a confidential moment that she knew one hundred and twenty-five different ways of kissing!"

"Oh, go on, Jim! She isn't the same woman!"

"Course she is. I can't make it out. What I think is the old man's cleared out and left her; that's all my eye about shearing. Sweet life! The only people who come through now are Maoris and sundowners!"

Through the dark we saw the gleam of the kid's pinafore. She trailed over to us with a basket in her hand, the milk billy in the other. I unpacked the basket, the child standing by.

"Come over here," said Jim, snapping his fingers at her.

She went, the lamp from the inside of the tent cast a bright light over her: a mean, undersized brat, with whitish hair and weak eyes. She stood, legs wide apart and her stomach protruding.

"What do you do all day?" asked Jim.

She scraped out one ear with her little finger, looked at the result and said, "Draw."

"Huh! What do you draw? Leave your ears alone!"

"Pictures."

"What on?"

"Bits of butter paper an' a pencil of my Mumma's."

"Boh! What a lot of words at one time!" Jim rolled his eyes at her. "Baa-lambs and moo-cows"

"No, everything. I'll draw all of you when you're gone, and your horses and the tent, and that one"—she pointed to me—"with no clothes on in the creek. I looked at her where she couldn't see me from."

"Thanks very much. How ripping of you," said Jim. "Where's Dad?"

The kid pouted. "I won't tell you because I don't like yer face." She started operations on the other ear.

"Here," I said. "Take the basket, get along home and tell the other man supper's ready."

"I don't want to."

"I'll give you a box on the ear if you don't," said Jim, savagely.

"Hie! I'll tell Mumma. I'll tell Mumma." The kid fled. We ate until we were full, and had arrived at the smoke stage before Joe came back, very flushed and jaunty, a whisky bottle in his hand.

"'Ave a drink you two!" he shouted, carrying off matters with a high hand. "'Ere, shove along the cups."

"One hundred and twenty-five different ways," I murmured to Jim.

"What's that? Oh! stow it!" said Joe. "Why 'ave you always got your knife into me? You gas like a kid at a Sunday School beano. She wants us to go up there tonight, and have a comfortable chat. I,"—he waved his hand airily—"I got 'er round."

"Trust you for that," laughed Jim. "But did she tell you where the old man's got to?"

Joe looked up. "Shearing! You 'eard 'er, you fool!"

The woman had fixed up the room, even to a light bouquet of sweet-williams on the table. She and I sat one side of the table, Joe and Jim the other. An oil lamp was set between us, the whisky bottle and glasses, and a jug of water. The kid knelt against one of the forms, drawing on butter paper. I wondered if she was attempting the creek episode. But Joe had been right about night time. The woman's hair was tumbled; two red spots burned in her cheeks; her eyes shone; and we knew that they were kissing feet under the table. She had changed the blue pinafore for a white calico dressing jacket and a black skirt; the kid was decorated to the extent of a blue sateen hair ribbon. In the stifling room, with the flies buzzing against the ceiling and dropping on to the table, we got slowly drunk.

"Now listen to me," shouted the woman, banging her fist on the table. "It's six years since I was married, and four miscarriages. I says to 'im, I says, what do you think I'm doin' up 'ere? If you was back at the coast, I'd 'ave you lynched for child murder. Over and over I tells 'im: You've broken my spirit and spoiled my looks, and wot for? That's wot I'm driving at." She clutched her head with her hands and stared round at us. Speaking rapidly, "Oh, some days. An' months of them! I 'ear them two words knockin' inside me all the time: 'Wot for!' And sometimes I'll be cooking the spuds an' I lifts the lid off to give 'em a prong and I 'ears, quite sudden again, 'Wot for!' Oh! I don't mean only the spuds and the kid—I mean—I mean," she hiccoughed—"You know what I mean, Mr. Joe."

"I do," said Joe, scratching his head.

"Trouble with me is," she leaned across the table, "He left me too much alone. When the coach stopped coming, sometimes he'd go away days, sometimes he'd go away weeks, and leave me ter look after the store. Back 'e'd come, pleased as Punch. 'Oh, 'allo,' 'e'd say. 'Ow are you gettin' on? Come and give us a kiss.' Sometimes I'd turn a bit nasty, and then 'e'd go off again, and if I took it all right, 'e'd wait till 'e could twist me round 'is finger, then 'e'd say, 'Well, so long, I'm off,' and do you think I could keep 'em? Not me!"

"Mumma," bleated the kid, "I made a picture of them on the 'ill, an' you an' me, an' the dog down below."

"Shut your mouth!" said the woman.

A vivid flash of lightening played over the room. We heard the mutter of thunder.

"Good thing that's broke lose," said Joe. "I've 'ad it in me 'ead for three days."

"Where's your old man now?" asked Jim, slowly.

The woman blubbered and dropped her head on to the table.

"Jim, 'e's gone shearin' and left me alone again," she wailed.

"'Ere, look out for the glasses," said Joe. "Cheer-o, 'ave another drop. No good cryin' over spilt 'usbands!"

"Mr. Joe," said the woman, drying her eyes on her jacket frill, "You're a gent, an' if I was a secret woman, I'd place any confidence in your 'ands. I don't mind if I do 'ave a glass of that."

Every moment the lighting grew more vivid and the thunder sounded nearer. Jim and I were silent; the kid never moved from her bench. She poked her tongue out and blew on her paper as she drew.

"It's the loneliness," said the woman, addressing Joe—he made sheep's eyes at her—"and bein' shut up 'ere like a broody 'en." He reached his hand across the table and held hers, and though the position looked most uncomfortable when they wanted to pass the water and whisky, their hands stuck together as though glued. I pushed back my chair and went over to the kid, who immediately sat flat down on her artistic achievements and made a face at me.

"You're not to look," said she.

"Oh, come on, don't be nasty!" Jim came over to us, and we were just drunk enough to wheedle the kid into showing us. And those drawings of hers were extraordinary and repulsively vulgar. The creations of a lunatic with a lunatic's cleverness. While she showed them to us, she worked herself up into a mad excitement, laughing and trembling, shooting out her arms.

"Mumma," she yelled. "Now I'm going to draw them what you told me I never was to. Now I am."

The woman rushed from the table and beat the child's head with the flat of her hand.

"I'll smack you with yer clothes turned up if yer dare say that again," she bawled.

Joe was too drunk to notice or care, but Jim caught her by the arm. The kid did not utter a cry. She drifted over to the window and began picking flies from the treacle paper.

We returned to the table: Jim and I sitting one side, the woman and Joe, touching shoulders, on the other. We listened to the thunder, saying stupidly, "That was a near one," "There it goes again," and Joe, at a heavy hit, "Now we're off," "Steady on the brake," until rain began to fall, sharp as cannon shot on the iron roof.

"You'd better doss here for the night," said the woman.

"That's right," assented Joe, evidently in the know about this move.

"Bring up yer things from the tent. You two can doss in the store along with the kid. She's used to sleep in there and won't mind you."

"Oh Mumma, I never did," interrupted the kid.

"Shut yer lies! An' Mr. Joe can 'ave this room."

It sounded a ridiculous arrangement, but it was useless to attempt to cross them, they were too far gone. While the woman sketched the plan of action, Joe sat, solemn and red, his eyes bulging, and pulling at his moustache.

"Give us a lantern," said Jim, "I'll go down to the paddock."

We two went together. Rain whipped in our faces; the land was light as though a bush fire was raging. We behaved like two children let loose in the thick of an adventure, laughed and shouted to each other, and came back to the whare to find the kid already bedded in the counter of the store. The woman brought us a lamp. Joe took his bundle from Jim, the door was shut.

"Good-night all," shouted Joe.

Jim and I sat on two sacks of potatoes. For the life of us we could not stop laughing. Strings of onions and half-hams dangled from the ceiling. Wherever we looked there were advertisements for "Camp Coffee" and tinned meats. We pointed at them, tried to read them aloud, overcome with laughter and hiccoughs. The kid in the counter stared at us. She threw off her blanket and scrambled to the floor, where she stood in her grey flannel nightgown, rubbing one leg against the other. We paid no attention to her.

"Wot are you laughing at?" she said, uneasily.

"You!" shouted Jim. "The red tribe of you, my child."

She flew into a rage and beat herself with her hands. "I won't be laughed at, you curs—you." He swooped down upon the child and swung her on to the counter.

"Go to sleep, Miss Smarty—or make a drawing—here's a pencil—you can use Mumma's account book."

Through the rain we heard Joe creak over the boarding of the next room—the sound of a door being opened, then shut to.

"It's the loneliness," whispered Jim.

"One hundred and twenty-five different ways, alas! My poor brother!"

The kid tore out a page and flung it at me.

"There you are," she said. "Now I done it ter spite Mumma for shutting me up 'ere with you two. I done the one she told me she'd shoot me if I did. Don't care! Don't care!"

The kid had drawn a picture of the woman shooting at a man with a rook rifle and then digging a hole to bury him in.

She jumped off the counter and squirmed about on the floor biting her nails.

Jim and I sat till dawn with the drawing beside us. The rain ceased, the little kid fell asleep, breathing loudly. We got up, stole out of the whare, down into the paddock. White clouds floated over a pink sky. A chill wind blew, and the air smelled of wet grass. Just as we swung into the saddle Joe came out of the whare. He motioned to us to ride on.

"I'll pick you up later," he shouted.

A bend in the road, and the whole place disappeared.

SUMMARY:

1. I rode through the hot New Zealand countryside with two companions, Joe and Jim. We were looking for comfort in our travels, headed for a store Jim knew about. The store, Jim said, was owned by a friend of his, his wife had yellow hair and a reputation for being more than friendly.

2. We came to the top of the hill, and the store, along with paddocks, was before us. The yellow-haired woman and her daughter greeted us. Her husband, she said, was away shearing. She certainly wasn't attractive, and not particularly friendly, but she said we could stay.

3. I followed her to her house to get some salve for the horses, discovering it unkempt, and the woman half-mad. She took forever to find the salve, then told me she'd fix us supper. I asked her about Else, the child—she was six, but had sickened as an infant when her mother's milk didn't come in—which accounted for her looking like a rat.

4. I took the salve to Jim and Joe in the paddock, and found Joe all dressed up. I went to bathe, and when I came back, Joe was gone. I asked Jim about the woman; he explained she had been pretty, and had once told him she knew 125 ways of kissing.

5. The kid came to the paddock with a billy of milk and supper; Jim asked her what she did, and she said she drew pictures.

6. Joe came back, and said the woman had invited us up for a chat. We sat in the mean room and drank whiskey, while the kid sat on the floor and drew. Joe and the woman flirted while we got drunk. The woman complained that her husband ruined her looks and left her alone too much, and she wondered, "Wot for?"

7. As Joe and the woman got friendly, I went over to look at the kid's drawings. She wouldn't show, instead telling her mother she was going to draw what she had been forbidden to draw. The mother whacked her.

8. A thunderstorm broke, and the woman said we should stay there the night. Jim and I shared a room with the child, Joe and the woman stayed in another room. We laughed for a while, teasing the kid, until she drew a picture at us, saying it was the one her mumma had forbidden her to draw.

9. The picture showed the woman shooting at a man, and digging a hole to bury him in.

10. We sat still until morning, then saddled up and prepared to ride out. Joe came out of the house, and motioned us to ride on. "I'll pick you up later," he shouted, as we rounded a bend and the place disappeared.

TEOTIHUACAN

by John Long

Teotihuacan, or *"Place of the Gods,"* was the first true city of Middle America. During its zenith around 300 AD, roughly 50,000 people occupied the exposed valley close to present-day Mexico City. Central to this agrarian society—which ebbed and flowed with the vagaries of weather—was their homage to the gods of rain (Tloloc) and spring (Xipe Totec), and the rituals enacted to win their favor. To this day the archaeologists dig and sift, and scholars add key shards to a prodigious puzzle; yet no one has fully explained how the great community disappeared around 700 AD. Only the pyramids survive the now-ancient necropolis.

She cannot remember Her mother's face. The priests came and took Her away after divining the marks on Her head that fated Her to this sacred day. As far back as memory takes Her, She has lived here in the cloister, has bowed before the gods of rain and spring whose renewed charity Teotihuacan so direly needs. The priestesses bicker and brood around Her, a few jealous, the rest relieved to be spared Her "honor" themselves. She has caught the animal fear surging in their eyes these last few days; but nothing can frighten Her faith away. All of Her seventeen years have passed preparing for this hour, and it has come. The oldest priestess kisses Her on the lips, then places a narrow crown, inlaid with jade and abalone shell, onto Her head. Her hair gleams like onyx from holy oils. Aside from the crown, She is naked.

A quarter mile north, a dozen priests dazzlingly plumed, their minds stretched by chanting and Morning Glory seeds, stumble from the small temple set on the flat-topped Pyramid Of The Sun, a colossal edifice of earth and bricks sheathed with diamond-bright limestone. The priests pause to take in the dry, open valley below them. Slowly, they start down the steep stone staircase, flanked every tenth step by stone snake heads, their jagged teeth barred, extending from a low wall running down the sloping sides of the pyramid. His neck crooked by the heavy crown and two-hundred feathers, the high priest leads the way; the others descend behind him like a chevron of exotic birds.

A door opens and the sunset gushes into the small cloister. She feels a great release, having lived behind closed doors for fifteen years. It is Her tribute to leave the cloister first, and She walks out toward the exploding sky with such poise and dignity that the more nervous of Her handlers realize the high priest was precisely right in choosing Her, and that the sacred day is requisite and true after all.

Just south, a second company of priests marches down the Pyramid of The Moon. At the bottom, the two groups meet, fall in behind Her, and proceed down the broad Calle de los Muertos (Avenue of the Dead) through the heart of the city. The calle is bordered by tall stone obelisks, graven with icons and towering in chiseled outline against the setting sun. In their shadows, a multitude—the thousands of peons and nobility of the great city—stand in noisy awe, none of it so great as Hers.

Nobody had told Her there were so many people in the world, or that all of them would turn out for Her great day. And nobody had told the multitude that She would walk past certain and superb, Her head held high. The effect stuns. Against the soft grace of Her frame, they feel the jagged edges of their lives. After days of prologues and blistering winds, the animal fear has every one of them by the throat. The closer She gets, the tighter the grip. It is at this fear that they cheer and abet, rant in tongues, weep in terror, stare gravely and say little or nothing.

The drought has made them this way, She thinks, and they feel I might fail them. But I am not afraid.

She marches on, indomitable. No one need help Her along, no one need drag Her, as the priests have so often had to do in the past. The hope in Her step rallies them, and what She sees beyond them rallies Her.

Directly off the calle looms a psychedelic ensemble of shrines to Tloloc and Xipe Totec, gods of rain and spring, others for los Subterraneos, and many more. They are harmoniously set between the homes of lesser priest/aristocrats, artisans and merchants. The orange clay roofs are supported by posts and wooden beams carved into giant reptiles and allegorical animals. The walls, covered in lime-plaster, are continuous frescos across which pass a cavalcade of priests, gods, jaguar-men and springing athletes locked in the fatal pelota game, all styled in gleaming whites, reds, greens, blues and yellows. She feels a rush of emptiness, realizing Her two-mile march is all She will ever see of Her people and their kingdom, the austere lines and magnificent distances of Teotihuacan.

The closer they draw to the Temple of Quetzalcoatl, the more the crowd drops away and the drums pick up. Finally, the 35,000 are behind them, and they enter a square enclosure walled with massive buildings: The Citadel. Instinct leads Her across black cobblestones toward the temple of the Feathered Serpent, ageless icon of the Mexican pantheon, the bringer of knowledge and civilization. Protruding from all sides of the temple-pyramid, enormous stone heads of the serpent alternate with the frightening Olmecesque face, flat and negroid, of the rain god Tloloc.

She moves to the steep stone staircase leading to the large flat crown of the pyramid, and starts up. With each step, She leaves more of Her life behind, until all that remains are the raw images, smells and sounds of La Calle de los Muertos and the pyramid itself, each face and icon, mote of incense and quickening drum cadence fighting for Her mind's attention. Her eyes are as dry as the air. She floats up the staircase, propelled by unseen hands.

The top. She turns to the west. The sky is on fire. Far below, reaching out from the calle and beyond, the great city holds its breath.

Long ago, the gods had gathered here after the sun had died. One by one they threw themselves into a fire so the sun would rise again and give light to the world. Now, on the threshold of the vernal equinox, it is time to reimburse Tloloc, god of rain. Gorged with sensations and images, She scarcely feels the two priests grab Her ankles, or the first bite of the obsidian knife slicing up the back of Her leg to the small of Her back. She feels the second pass up the other leg, and the deep slash up Her spine and over the top of Her head; and all at once the animal fear springs on Her. But true to Her end, She fights to hold the whole exploding expanse in Her eyes. The colors run together and wax greyer and darker and finally set off the edge of Her mind.

To beckon Xipe Totec, god of spring and deliverer of crops, the high priest will strip Her skin off in one piece, don it as a robe and dance around the alter to hasten the rains and celebrate the coming Spring, when nature puts on a fresh young coat of vegetation. The dreadful fealty of the gods now appeased, the priests will descend the pyramid to stare mutely at the sky and wait. She, but a lump of carrion, will be left for a gyre of ravens circling in the thermals above the pyramid.

Soon the sky will darken and snarl, the rains will fall, and new life will burst through the stony earth. In time, the sun will again fill the sky and will turn Her bones to dust, which arid winds will blow into great rivers that wash into the deltas and into the ocean, where She will mingle with the deep and range over the face of the entire world. Her journey will outlive Tloloc, and no ashes could be strewn more thoroughly, nor a shrine exist more lasting, than the pyramids of Teotihuacan.

SUMMARY:

1. She is prepared by priestesses for Her sacred day, which She was chosen for as a small child. She can't remember Her mother; She has never left the temple.

2. In the temple to the north, a dozen priests prepare for the ceremony, then emerge from the Pyramid of the Sun, descending the broad stone staircase that climbs the front of the pyramid upon which the temple stands.

3. In the temple to the south, the Pyramid of the Moon, another group of priests makes its preparations, then desends the pyramid.

4. The doors to Her cloister open, and She sees the outside for the first time in fifteen years. Beneath the hot sun, She sees thousands of people have gathered, and she sees the great city of Teotihuacan for the first time.

5. She is met by the two groups of priests, who fall in behind Her, and they proceed down the Calle de

los Muertos (Avenue of the Dead) through the heart of the city, which blisters under the heat.

6. The people watch Her; they have been made jagged and harried by the drought. She passes into a complex of shrines to the gods of spring and rain.

7. She comes to The Citadel and mounts the Pyramid, which is decorated with the faces of Tloloc, the rain god.

8. She reached the top and turns to face the sun. It is the vernal equinox, the time to reimburse Tloloc, who will give the people rain.

9. She is dazzled by the rising sun, and so does not feel the first cuts of the knife. As terror siezes Her, the high priest finishes his grisly duty, stripping off her skin and wearing it like a robe to appease the gods of spring and rain.

10. The rain comes and washes Her dried bones out to sea, where Her journey will outlast the reign of Tloloc, and the pyramids of Teotihuacan.

WHERE THERE'S A WILL

by *Richard Matheson and*
Richard Christian Matheson

He awoke.

It was dark and cold. And silent.

I'm thirsty, he thought. He yawned and sat up, hit his head on something and fell back with a cry of pain. He rubbed at the pulsing tissue on his brow, feeling the ache spread back to his hairline. Slowly, he tried sitting up again but hit his head once more. He was jammed between the mattress and something above. He raised his hands to feel something, soft and pliable, yield to the push of his fingers. He felt along its surface, which extended as far as he could reach. He swallowed anxiously and shivered. What in God's name was it?

He began to roll to his left and stopped with a gasp. The surface was blocking him. He reached to his right and his heart beat faster. He was surrounded on all four sides.

Within seconds, he sensed that he was dressed. He felt trousers, a coat, a shirt and tie, a belt. There were shoes on his feet. He slid his right hand into his trouser pocket and palmed a cold, metal square. He pulled his hand from the pocket, bringing it to his face. Fingers trembling, he hanged the top open and spun the wheel with his thumb. A few sparks glinted but no flame. Another turn and it lit. He looked down at the orange cast of his body and shivered again.

He was in a casket.

He dropped the lighter and the flame striped the air with a yellow tracer before going out. Total darkness once more. His terrified breathing lurched from his throat. How long had he been here? Minutes? Hours?

His hopes lunged at the possibility that he was only dreaming, his sleeping mind caught in a hideous nightmare. But he knew it wasn't so. He knew, horribly enough, that they had put him in the one place he was most terrified of, the one place he had made the fatal mistake of speaking about to them. They couldn't have selected a better torture had they pondered it for a hundred years. God, did they loathe him that much? To do this to him?

He started shaking helplessly, then caught himself. He wouldn't let them do it. Take his life and his business all at once? No, goddamn them, no!

He searched hurriedly for the lighter. That was their mistake, he thought. On the lighter were the words: "To Charlie Where there's a Will…" Stupid bastards. They probably thought it was a final, fitting irony: A gold-engraved thank you for making the corporation what it was.

"Right," he muttered. He'd beat the lousy sons of bitches. They weren't going to murder him and steal the business he owned and built. There was a will. His.

He closed his fingers around the lighter and lifted it above his heaving chest. The wheel ground against the flint as he spun it back with his thumb: the flame caught and he surveyed what space he had in the coffin—only inches on all four sides. How much air could there be in so small a space, he wondered? He clicked off the lighter. Don't burn it up, he told himself. Work in the dark.

He tried to push the lid up, pressing hard as he could, his forearms straining. He pounded his fists against the lid until his hands throbbed and sweat beaded on his forehead. The lid remained fixed. He reached into his left trouser pocket and pulled out a chain with two keys attached. They had placed those with him, too. Stupid bastards. Did they really think he'd be so terrified he couldn't think? He wouldn't need the keys to his car and to the office again so why not put them in the casket with him? Wrong. He would use them again.

Just before his face, he began to pick at the lining with the sharp edge of one key, tearing through the threads and ripping apart the material. He pulled at it with his fingers until it popped free from its fastenings. Working quickly, he pulled the downy stuff away and placed it at his sides. He tried not to breathe too hard, to save the air.

He flicked on the lighter and looking at the cleared area, knocked against it with the knuckles of his free hand. Oak, not metal. "Stupid bastards," he muttered, smiling slightly. Another mistake on their part. No mystery why he had always been so far ahead of them.

Gripping the keys together firmly, he began digging them against the oak. The flame of the lighter shook as he watched small pieces of the lid being chewed off by the gouging of the keys. Splinter after splinter fell. The lighter kept going out and he had to spin the flint over and over, repeating each move, until his hands felt numb. Fearing that he would use up the air, he turned the lighter off again, and continued to chisel at the wood, falling on his neck and chin. His arm began to ache.

He was losing strength. Wood no longer came off as steadily. He laid his keys on his chest and flicked on the lighter again: he could see a tattered path of wood where he had dug but it was only inches long. Not enough, he thought. It's not enough.

He slumped and took a deep breath, stopping halfway through. The air was thinning. He reached up and pounded against the lid.

"Open this thing, goddammit," he shouted, the veins in his neck rising beneath the skin, "Open this thing and let me out!"

I'll die if I don't do something more, he thought. They'll win. His face tightened. He had never given up before. Never. And they weren't going to win. There was no way to stop him once he made up his mind. He'd show those bastards what willpower was.

Quickly, he took the lighter in his right hand and turned the wheel several times. The flame rose like a streamer, fluttering back and forth before his eyes. Steadying his left arm with his right, he held the flame to the wood and began to scorch the ripped grain.

He breathed in short, shallow breaths now, wincing at the reek of butane and scorched wood as it filled the casket. The lid began to speckle with tiny sparks as he ran the flame along the gouge. He held it to one spot for several moments then slid it to another spot, the wood making faint crackling sounds.

Suddenly, a flame formed on the surface of the wood. He coughed as the burning oak gave off motes of grey pulpy smoke. The air continued to thin and he felt his lungs working against the gummy fumes. He felt as though he might faint and his body began to lose feeling.

Desperately, he tore away part of his shirt and wrapped it around his right hand and wrist. A section of the lid was beginning to char and had become brittle. He slammed his swathed fist and forearm against the smoking wood and it crumbled down on him, glowing embers falling on his face and neck. He scrambled frantically to slap them out. Several burned his chest and palms and he cried out in pain.

Now a portion of the lid had become a glowing skeleton of wood, the heat radiating downward at his face. He squirmed away from it, turning his head to avoid the falling embers. The casket was filled with smoke and he could breathe only the choking, burning smell of it. His throat was hot and raw. Fine-powder ash filled his mouth and nose as he pounded at the lid with his wrapped fist. "Come on!" he screamed.

The section of the lid gave suddenly and fell in around him. He slapped at his face, neck and chest but the hot particles sizzled on his skin and he had to bear the pain as he tried to smother them.

The embers began to darken, one by one, and now he smelled something new and strange. He searched for the lighter at his side, found it, and flicked it on.

Moist, root-laden soil packed firmly overhead.

Reaching up, he ran his fingers across it. In the flickering light, he saw burrowing insects and great white earthworms, dangling inches from his face. He drew down as far as he could, pulling his face from their wriggling movements.

Unexpectedly, one of the larva pulled free and dropped. It fell to his face and its jelly-like casing stuck to his upper lip. He thrust both hands upward, digging at the soil. He shook his head wildly to throw the larva off. He continued to dig, the dirt falling in on him. It poured into his nose and he could hardly breathe. It stuck to his lips and slipped into his mouth. He closed his eyes tightly but could feel it clumping on the lids. He held his breath as he pistoned his hands upward and forward like a digging machine gone amok. He eased his body up, a little at a time, letting the dirt collect under him. His lungs were laboring, dying for air. He didn't dare open his eyes. His fingers became raw from digging, nails bent backward on several fingers, breaking off. He couldn't even feel the pain or the running blood but knew the dirt was stained red by its flow. The pain in his arms and lungs grew worse with each second. But he continued to press himself upward, pulling his feet and knees closer to his chest, wrestling into a kind of fetal crouch, hands above his head, upper arms gathered around his face. He clawed fiercely at the dirt, which gave way with each shovelling gouge of his fingers. Keep going, he told himself. Keep going. He refused to stop and die in the earth. He bit down hard, his teeth nearly breaking from the tension of his jaws. Keep going, he thought. Keep going!

He pushed up harder and harder, dirt cascading over his body, gathering in his hair and on his shoulders. Filth surrounded him. His lungs felt to burst. It seemed like minutes since he had taken a breath. He wanted to scream, but couldn't. His naked cuticles grated against the compact dirt. His mouth opened in pain and was filled with moist earth, covering his tongue and gathering in his throat. He retched, vomit and dirt mixing as it exploded from his mouth. His head began to empty of life as he felt himself breathing in more dirt. The dirt clogged in his throat, and his heart pounded. I'm losing! he thought in anguish.

Suddenly, one finger thrust up through the crust of earth. Unthinkingly, he moved his hand like a trowel and drove it through to the surface. His arms suddenly went crazy, pulling and punching at the dirt until an opening expanded. He kept thrashing at the opening, his entire system glutted with dirt. His chest felt as if it would tear down the middle.

Then his arms were poking out of the grave and within several seconds he had pulled his upper body from the ground. He kept pulling, hooking his shredded fingers into the earth and sliding his legs from the hole. They yanked out and he lay on the ground completely, gasping. But no air could get through the dirt which had collected in his windpipe and mouth. He writhed, turning on his back and side until he'd finally raised himself to a forward kneel and began hacking phlegm-covered mud from his air passages. Black saliva ran down his chin as he continued to throw up violently, dirt exploding from his mouth to the ground. When most of it was out he began to gasp, as oxygen rushed into his chest, cool air filling his body with life.

I've won, he thought. I've beaten the bastards, beaten them! He began to laugh hysterically till he pried his eyes open and looked around, rubbing at his blood-covered lids. He heard the sound of traffic and blinding lights glared at him. They crisscrossed his face, rushing at him from left and right. He winced, struck dumb by their glare, then realized where he was.

The cemetery by the highway.

Cars and trucks roared back and forth, tires humming. He breathed a sigh at being near life again, near movement and people. A grunting smile raised his lips.

Looking to his right, he saw a gas station sign high on a metal pole several hundred yards up the highway. Struggling to his feet, he ran. As he did, he made a plan: Go to the gas station, wash up in the rest room, then borrow a dime and call for a limo from the company to come and get him. No. Better a cab. That way he could fool those sons of bitches. Catch them by surprise. They undoubtedly assumed he was long gone by now. Well, he had beat them. He knew it as he picked up the pace of his run. Nobody could stop you when you really wanted something, he told himself, glancing back in the direction of the grave he had just escaped. He ran into the station from the back and made his way to the bathroom. He didn't want anyone to see his dirtied, bloodied state.

There was a pay phone in the bathroom and he locked the door before plowing into his pockets for change. He found two pennies and a quarter and deposited the silver coin. They'd even provided him with money. Stupid bastards.

He dialed his wife.

She answered and screamed when he told her what had happened. She screamed and screamed. What a hideous joke she said. Whoever was doing this was a heartless monster. She hung up before he could stop her. He dropped the phone and turned to face the bathroom mirror.

He could only stare in silence. Staring back at him was a face that was missing sections of flesh. Its skin was grey, and withered yellow bone showed through on his chin and one cheek.

Then he remembered what else his wife had said and began to weep: It had been over seven months, she'd said. Seven months.

SUMMARY:

1. He awoke cold and thirsty. He yawned, and tried to get up, but bumped his head on something. He rolled over, and found himself boxed in. Unable

to see in the dark, he fumbled for his lighter. In the flickering light, he realized his worst fear had come true—he is trapped in a casket.

2. Could his business partners have loathed him enough to do this, he wondered. Well, he wouldn't let them get away with it. He'd get out.

3. He found his keys in his pocket, and began picking away at the lining of the coffin. Eventually he got through that, fighting his terror all the while, and began digging at the oak of the coffin lid.

4. The air began to thin, and he became more desperate. After a moment of panic, he applied the lighter to the wood, which began to burn, filling the casket with smoke.

5. He ripped off a piece of his shirt, wrapped it around his hand, and pounded a hole through the oak, only to find moist, root-laden soil above.

6. He began to dig through the dirt, wiping away the dirt and larva that cascaded in on him with the soil. Slowly, he began to lose his air, and clawed his way frantically toward the surface.

7. Just as his lungs failed, a finger poked through the surface. He was free. He unburied himself completely, discovering he had been buried in the cemetery by the highway.

8. He found his way to a gas station, where he ducked into the bathroom to fix himself up. There was a pay phone inside—he found a quarter in his pants, and called his wife.

9. She panicked on the phone, screaming that it was a dirty trick. She hung up, and he, shocked at her

reaction, looked at himself in the bathroom mirror. A withered, grey, partially fleshless face stared back at him.

10. His wife had been screaming that her husband had been dead more than seven months.

"THE DIRTY NINCOMPOOP WHO EDITS THAT JOURNAL"

*F*rontier newspaper editors raised vituperation to a fine art—especially when lambasting one another. The following examples are from the Weekly Arizona Miner, edited by John Marion at Prescott, and the Arizona Sentinel, edited by Judge William J. Berry at Yuma. The fact that the two men were old friends did not moderate the language.

In the daily issue of [The Arizona "Miner"] this most scurrilous sheet of October 27th, we find an article in reference to ourself, which is altogether characteristic of the dirty nincompoop who edits that journal.

We shall not attempt to reply sciatim to the charge brought against us in said article, but will simply say that it is a batch of infernal false-hoods from beginning to end. The vile wretch who edits the *Miner* and who wrote that article, well knows, as every man in Arizona knows (who ever saw or heard him), that he is nothing if not a blackguard. He accuses us of being a gunsmith. We are proud of that, as many a man in Arizona will attest that we are a good one. Likewise we are a better editor and a better and more respectable man than he is which incontrovertible fact is well known. He charges us with demanding high prices for our gunsmith work. To that we say that we never got as much as our work was worth, and lost to the tune of fifteen hundred dollars by trusting certain treacherous scoundrels in Prescott and vicinity.

The miserable liar also says he let us write a communication for the *Miner*, years ago. Why, the shameless mongrel used to beg us to write for his foul abortion, and since we quit writing for it, many Arizonians say that the *Miner* is not worth a damn, and that is our opinion too, though we never expressed it publically before. Marion says we used to reside "up in *Osegon*!" Where is Osegon? (*sic*) We would like to know.

In regard to our being a "judge of whisky," we will simply say that no man ever saw Judge Wm. J. Berry laid out under its influence; while we had the extreme mortification of seeing the editor of the *Miner*, in a party given by Col. Baker in Prescott, laid out in the refreshment room, dead drunk, with candles placed at his head and feet, and a regular "wake" held over him.

As he lay, with drunken slobber issuing from his immence mouth, which extends from ear to ear, and his ears reaching up so high, everyone present was forcibly impressed with the fact that we had discovered the connecting link between the catfish and the jackass. What we have here faintly described is the truth, to attest which there are plenty of living witnesses. Now dry up, or we will come out with some more reminiscences.

(*Arizona Sentinel* of Nov. 7, 1874)

When two editors have such vivid personalities, each wants the last word. Since there is no pressing business at the time, a good fight adds sparkle to an infrequent moment of calm in the territory. Marion then replies to Berry's latest editorial with:

We had intended to let the mammouth ape whose name appears as editor of the *Yuma Sentinel* severely alone, until a day or two ago a citizen of Prescott requested us to inform our readers that Berry uttered a gratuitous falsehood when he stated that "he lost $1,500 by trusting certain treacherous scoundrels in Prescott and vicinity."

This being a reasonable and legitimate request, we now assert that Berry lied when he said so, and that it would take more than $1,500 to pay for the whisky which Berry "bummed" during his long sojourn in Prescott, not to speak of that which he guzzled in our sister city of Mohave, previous to the day upon which he found himself debarred from the privilege of swallowing whisky in Cerbat.

Again, we have been asked our reasons for not disputing certain assertions of his, regarding ourself. Well, one reason is: Berry is a natural and artificial liar, whom nobody was ever known to believe. Then, he did tell one truth about us, i.e., that drink once got the better of us. We were drunk that night, and have never yet attempted to deny it. But, Berry drank ten times to our once, and the only reason that he did not fall down and crawl on all fours like the cur that he is, was that there was not sufficient liquor in the house to fill his hogshead. Berry says no one ever saw him get drunk. When he lived in Prescott his first great care was to freight himself with whisky, after which it was his custom to walk like the swine that he is, on all fours, to his den.

He cannot have forgotten his visit to Lynx Creek, in 1864, when he rolled over a pine log, dead drunk, and served a useful purpose for a jacose man. Yes, Judge, we own up to that little drunk of ours; but unlike you, we were not pointed out and derided as a whisky bloat; nor did any person ever attempt to use us as a water-closet, as you were used that day on Lynx Creek.

As to your being a better editor than the writer of this, it is for the public to judge, not for you to assert, although you asserted it.

You have called us a blackguard, regardless of the old story about the kettle.

Then you have accused us of toadying to Gen. Cook; you, who have toadied and bent your knees to every placeholder, capitalist and bar-keeper in this section of Arizona; you, who made an egregious ass of yourself by firing an anvil salute in honor of Gen. Stoneman, who, you will recollect, never acknowledged the "honor done him." And you, who take up the cudgels for thieving Indian agents and, by doing so, go back on your record, made when you used to write and speak against the "Indian Ring Robbers and Murderers."

Ah, Judge, you have many masters; have been everything (except an independent man) by turns and nothing long. Had you changed shirts as often as you changed masters, there would be one sand-bar less in the Colorado River, and we would not know that you were in Yuma when, according to your published statement, you should be in San Francisco.

Hoping that these few lines will find you drunk and obedient to your masters, as usual, we say in our "classic" language, "uncork and be damned."

(*Arizona Miner* of Jan. 5, 1875)

91

THE END OF THE DUEL

by Jorge Luis Borges

Manuel Cardoso and Carmen Silveira had a few acres of land that bordered each other. Like the roots of other passions, those of hatred are mysterious, but there was talk of a quarrel over some unbranded cattle or a free-for-all horse race in which Silveira, who was the stronger of the two, had run Cardoso's horse off the edge of the trail. Months afterward, a long two-handed game of truco of thirty points took place in the local saloon. Following almost every hand, Silveira congratulated his opponent on his skill, but in the end left him without a cent. When he tucked his winnings away in his money belt, Silveira thanked Cardoso for the lesson he had been given. It was then, I believe, that they were at the point of having it out. But the onlookers, who were quite a few, separated them. A peculiar twist of the story is that Manuel Cardoso and Carmen Silveira must have run across each other out in the hills on more than one occasion, but they never actually faced each other until the very end. Maybe their poor and monotonous lives held nothing else for them than their hatred, and that was why they nursed it. In the long run, without suspecting it, each of the two became a slave to the other.

Cardoso, less out of love than out of boredom, took up with a neighbor girl, La Serviliana. That was all that Silveira had to find out, and, after his manner, he began courting her and brought her to his shack. A few months later, finding her in the way, he threw her out. Full of spite, the woman tried to seek shelter at Cardoso's. Cardoso spent one night with her, and by the next moon packed her off. He did not want the other man's leavings.

It was around the same time that the incident of Silveira's sheepdog took place. Silveira was very fond of the animal, and had named him Treinta y Tres, after Uruguay's thirty-three founding fathers. When the dog was found dead in a ditch, Silveira was quick to suspect who had poisoned it.

Sometime during the winter of 1870, a civil war broke out between the Colorados or Reds, who were in power, and Aparicio's Blancos, or Whites. The revolution found Silveira and Cardoso in the same crossroads saloon where they had played their game of cards. A Brazilian half-breed, at the head of a detachment of gaucho militiamen, harangued all those present, telling them that the country needed them and that the government oppression was unbearable. He handed around white badges to mark them as Blancos, and at the end of his speech, which nobody understood, everyone in the place was rounded up. They were not even allowed to say goodbye to their families.

Manuel Cardoso and Carmen Silveira accepted their fate; a soldier's life was no harder than a gaucho's. Sleeping in the open on their sheepskin saddle blankets was something to which they were already hardened, and as for killing men, that held no difficulty for hands already in the habit of killing cattle. The clinking of stirrups and weapons is one of the things always heard when cavalry enters into action. The man who is not wounded at the outset thinks himself invulnerable. A lack of imagination freed Cardoso and Silveira from fear and from pity, although once in awhile, heading a charge, fear brushed them. They were never homesick. The idea of patriotism was alien to them, and, in spite of the badges they wore on their hats, one party was to them the same as the other. During the course of marches and countermarches, they learned what a man could do with a spear, and they found out that being companions allowed them to go on being enemies. They fought shoulder to shoulder and, for all we know, did not exchange a single word.

It was in the sultry fall of 1871 that a fight, which would not last an hour, happened in a place whose name they never knew. (Such places are later named by historians.) On the eve of the battle, Cardoso crept on all fours into his officer's tent and asked him sheepishly would he save him one of the Reds if the Whites won the next day, because up till then he had not cut anyone's throat and he wanted to know what it was like. His superior promised him that if he handled himself like a man he would be granted that favor.

The Whites outnumbered the enemy, but the Reds were better equipped and cut them down from the crown of a hill. After two unsuccessful charges that never reached the summit, the Whites' commanding officer, badly wounded, surrendered. On the very spot, at his own request, he was put to death by the knife.

The men laid down their arms. Captain Juan Patricio Nolan, who commanded the Reds, arranged the expected execution of the prisoners down to the last detail. He was from Cerro Largo himself, and knew all about the old rivalry between Silveira and Cardoso. He sent for the pair and told them, "I already know you two can't stand the sight of each other, and that for some time now you've been looking for the chance to have it out. I have good news for you. Before sundown, the two of you are going to have that chance to show who's the better man. I'm going to stand you up and have your throats cut, and then you'll run a race. God knows who'll win." The soldier who had brought them took them away.

It was not long before the news had spread throughout the camp. Nolan had made up his mind that the race would close the proceedings, but the prisoners sent him a representative to tell him that they, too, wanted to be spectators and to place wagers on the outcome. Nolan, who was an understanding man, let himself be convinced. The bets were laid down—money, riding gear, spears, sabers, horses. In due time they would be handed over to the widows or next of kin. The heat was unusual. So that no one would miss his siesta, things were delayed until four o'clock. Nolan, in the South American style, kept them waiting another hour. He was probably discussing the campaign with his officers, his aide shuttling in and out with the mate kettle.

Both sides of the dirt road in front of the tents were lined with prisoners, who, to make things easier, squatted on the ground with their hands tied behind their backs. A few of them relieved their feelings in a torrent of swearwords. One went over and over the Lord's Prayer. Almost all were stunned. Of course, they could not smoke. They no longer cared about the race now, but they all watched.

"They'll be cutting my throat on me, too," one of them said, showing his envy.

"Sure, but along with the mob," said his neighbor.

"Same as you," the first man snapped back.

With his saber, a sergeant drew a line in the dust across the road. Silveira's and Cardoso's wrists had been untied so that they could run freely. A space of some five yards was between them. Each man toed the mark. A couple of the officers asked the two not to let them down because everyone had placed great faith in them, and the sums they had bet on them came to quite a pile.

It fell to Silveira's lot to draw as executioner the mulatto Nolan, whose forefathers had no doubt been slaves of the captain's family and therefore bore his name. Cardoso drew the Reds' official cutthroat, a man from Corrientes well along in years, who, to comfort a condemned man, would pat him on the shoulder and tell him, "Take heart, friend. Women go through far worse when they give birth."

Their torsos bent forward, the two eager men did not look at each other. Nolan gave the signal.

The mulatto, swelling with pride to be at the center of attention, overdid his job and opened a showy slash that ran from ear to ear; the man from Corrientes did his with a narrow slit. Spurts of blood gushed from the men's throats. They dashed forward a number of steps before tumbling face down. Cardoso, as he fell, stretched out his arms. Perhaps never aware of it, he had won.

SUMMARY:

1. Maneul Cardoso and Carmen Silveira were neighbors, but had been enemies for many years.

2. The cause of the feud was obscure, but there were rumors of a horse race where Silveira had run Cardoso's horse off the course, and a card game in which Silveira had been cleaned out by Cardoso; they had to be separated to keep a brawl from breaking out.

3. There also was a contest for the love of a woman—in which the woman ended up the loser—and suspicions about the poisoning of Silveira's beloved dog.

4. Eventually, a civil war broke out. Silveira and Cardoso happened to be in a bar when a revolutionary, or White, came in and forceably recruited

all those present. They didn't even have time to say good-by to their families.

5. After many battles, in which the two men fought side by side but did not exchange a word, the Whites were finally defeated by the government forces, known as the Reds.

6. The Red commander organized the execution of all the prisoners. He knew of the feud between Cardoso and Silveira, as he was from the same town, and sent for them.

7. He would give them a chance to settle their feud once and for all, he told them. At sundown, their throats would be slit, and then they would run a race.

8. News of the contest spread quickly, and bets were made. The winnings of those who were destined to die would be sent on to their families.

9. Finally, time for the execution came. The men toed the line that had been scratched in the dirt. The executioners drew their knives across the men's necks and, blood spurting forth from the wounds, they lurched forward a number of steps.

10. As he fell, Cardoso stretched out his arms. He may never have known it, but he had won.

THE SHARK'S PARLOR

by James Dickey

Memory: I can take my head and strike it on a wall   on Cumberland
    Island
Where the night tide came crawling under the stairs   came up the first
Two or three steps   and the cottage stood on the poles all night
With the sea sprawled under it   as we dreamed of the great fin circling
Under the bedroom floor. In daylight there was my first brassy taste of
    beer
And Payton Ford and I came back from the Glynn County
    slaughterhouse
With a bucket of entrails and blood. We tied one end of a hawser
To a spindling porch pillar and rowed straight out of the house
Three hundred yards into the vast front yard of windless blue water
The rope outslithering its coil   the two-gallon jug stoppered and
    sealed
With wax   and a ten-foot chain leader   a drop-forged shark hook
    nestling.
We cast our blood on the waters   the land blood easily passing
For sea blood   and we sat in it for a moment with the stain spreading
Out from the boat   sat in a new radiance   in the pond of blood in
    the sea
Waiting for fins   waiting to spill our guts also in the glowing water.
We dumped the bucket, and baited the hook with a run-over collie pup.
    The jug
Bobbed, trying to shake off the sun as a dog would shake off the sea.
We rowed to the house   feeling the same water lift the boat a new way,
All the time seeing where we lived rise and dip with the oars.
We tied up and sat down in the rocking chairs, one eye or the other
    responding
To the blue-eye wink of the jug. Payton got us a beer and we sat
All morning sat there with blood on our minds   the red mark out
In the harbor slowly failing us   then   the house groaned   the rope

97

The Shark'sParlor

Sprang out of the water   splinters flew   we leapt from our chairs
And grabbed the rope   hauled   did nothing   the house coming
    subtly
Apart   all around us   underfoot   boards beginning to sparkle
    like sand
With the glinting of the bright hidden parts of ten-year-old nails
Pulling out   the tarred poles we slept propped-up on   leaning to sea
As in land wind   crabs scuttling from under the floor   as we took
    turns about
Two more porch pillars   and looked out and saw   something
    a fish-flash
An almighty fin in trouble   a moiling of secret forces   a false start
Of water   a round wave growing: in the whole of Cumberland
    Sound the one ripple.
Payton took off without a word I could not hold him either

But clung to the rope anyway it: it was the whole house bending
Its nail that held whatever it was   coming in a little and little a fool
I took up the slack on my wrist. The rope drew gently   jerked   I lifted
Clean off the porch and hit the water   the same water it was in
I felt in blue blazing terror at the bottom of the stairs and scrambled
Back up looking desperately into the human house as deeply as I could
Stopping my gaze before it went out the wire screen of the back door
Stopped it on the thistled rattan   the rugs I lay on and read
On my mother's sewing basket with next winter's socks spilling from it
The flimsy vacation furniture   a bucktoothed picture of myself
Payton came back with three men from a filling station   and glanced
    at me
Dripping water   inexplicable   then we all grabbed hold like a
    tug-of-war.

We were gaining a little   from us a cry went up   from everywhere
People came running. Behind us the house filled with men and boys.
On the third step from the sea I took my place   looking down the rope
Going into the ocean, humming and shaking off drops. A houseful
Of people put their backs into it   going up the steps from me

Into the living room   through the kitchen   down the back stairs
Up and over a hill of sand   across a dust road   and onto a raised
     field
Of dunes   we were gaining   the rope in my hands began to wet
With deeper water   all other haulers retreated through the house
But Payton and I on the stairs   drawing hand over hand on our blood
Drawing into existence by the nose   a huge body   becoming
A hammerhead   rolling in beery shadows   and I began to let up
But the rope still strained behind me   the town had gone
Pulling-mad in our house: far away in a field of sand they struggled
They had turned their backs on the sea   bent double   some on
     their knees
The rope over their shoulders like a bag of gold   they strove for the
     ideal
Esso station across the scorched meadow   with the distant fish
     coming up
The front stairs   the sagging board   still coming in   up   taking
Another step   toward the empty house   where the rope stood
     straining
By itself through the rooms   in the middle of the air. "Pass the word,"
Payton said, and I screamed it: "Let up, good God, let up!"   to no
     one there
The shark flopped on the porch, grating with salt-sand   driving
     back in
The nails he had pulled out   coughing chunks of his formless blood.
The screen door banged and tore off   he scrambled on his tail   slid
Curved   did a thing from another world   and was out of his
     element and in
Our vacation paradise   cutting all four legs from under the dinner
     table
With one deep-water move   he unwove the rugs in a moment
     throwing pints
Of blood over everything we owned   knocked the buck teeth out of
     my picture
His odd head full of crushed jelly-glass splinters and radio tubes
     thrashing

The Shark'sParlor

Among the pages of fan magazines   all the movie stars drenched in
     sea-blood.
Each time we thought he was dead   he struggled back and smashed
One more thing   in all coming back to die   three or four more
     times after death.
At last we got him out   log-rolling him   greasing his sandpaper skin
With lard to slide him   pulling on his chained lips as the tide came
Tumbled him down the steps as the first night wave went under the
     floor.
He drifted off   head back   belly white as the moon. What could I
     do but buy
That house   for the one black mark still there   against death   a
     forehead-
toucher in the room he circles beneath   and has been invited to
     wreck?
Blood hard as iron on the wall   black with time   still bloodlike
Can be touched whenever the brow is drunk enough: all changes:
     Memory:
Something like three-dimensional dancing in the limbs   with age
Feeling more in two worlds than one   in all worlds the growing
     encounters.

BECOMING NOTHING

by John Long

Drumming his crutches on the floor, Phil Chambers looked past an old man pressed against the window as the bus wound and chugged its way through Little Tokyo, the textile district, past the curbside row of towering palms shuddering in the smog. Since leaving the hospital, an annoying tick had started between his left eye and the corner of his mouth, a thing not lost on the leering old man at the window.

"Fairfax," droned the bus driver, the long metal vessel shimmying to a halt. Phil teetered out the rear exit and the bus roared off. The top of the Pogue Professional Building was visible on the skyline, several blocks north, and Phil thought he could get there at one go. Two blocks later, he sank onto a stone bench, trying desperately to execute the tantric breathing the monks had tried to teach him in Bhutan. Bhutan, known to its people as *Druk Yul*, "Land of the Thunder Dragon." How he wished he had never heard of that name, of that terrible, magnificent land.

Following their epic descent off Chomolari, Phil and climbing partner Dennis Rawls had staggered and crawled back to the Tak Sang monastery in the western shadow of the mountain. Three weeks before, the monks had warned them not to venture onto the sacred peak. Now frozen, more dead than alive, they were nursed by the monks, who did the best they could. Two months later, it all seemed like a vision from a fevered dream: The rarefied air, thick with heady incense and smoldering yak dung; the wildly costumed dancers, with masks of smiling demons, who performed for their welfare the "Dance of the Judgement of the Dead;" all the baffling rituals and gongs and spinning prayer wheels; and the unremitting dirges, basso-roars from the basement of time. Finally believing the climbers were purified, the head monk tried to teach them how to breathe. Through patois and shared intuition, they were made to understand that this breathing was their only hope of hanging on in the world.

Phil straightened on the bench and tried to visualize his breath making a circular passage—through his nose, down his windpipe, into his chest and back out—sucking in new life and exhaling all the naked fear that now ruled him. "Relax," he started. "I will relax, I will relax, I *am* relaxed," he chanted over and over, till he finally gave up and pulled a smoke from his pocket. He lit the cigarette, glanced at the words on the match box he'd found on the bus—"Nothing is forgotten, just forgiven"—and felt the familiar yet alien force pulling at the core of him.

"Christ," he mumbled out through gritted teeth. Every time his old fearless self would find its footing, this strange, shadowy force would strike him like a wrecking ball.

Phil knew that eventually, despair was the cost of impossible goals. He'd seen climber after climber venture off to defy another "unclimbable" mountain. Many would win, would return; but if they kept pushing it, a serac eventually would crush them dead or a sudden storm would freeze them to ice as sure as the monsoon blows. This crazy daring was the only blasphemy, yet an evil or weak man would never attempt it. Hope runs eternal for the mundane dreamer, because he never reaches the freezing-point of total failure. Phil Chambers was freezing to death. Not because he had failed, but because he had won, and was losing still.

"Christ."

He quickly teetered back onto his crutches and pressed on toward his destination, gaining it ten minutes later: Harlan K. Lassiter, General Psychiatry, read the sign on the big brown office door. Phil struggled through, and the secretary led him into Harlan's private study.

"Dr. L speaks highly of you," the secretary said, taking Phil's crutches and helping him into a high-backed leather chair. She probably knows about my toes, Phil thought; and the bandages tell the story if she doesn't. Her contrite smile angered him in any event. "He's proud of you, really," she added. "Sounds like he's a right to be." Harlan must have told her about my ludicrous accomplishments, Phil thought, and grew angrier still.

"Harlan's got too much pride," Phil said, "Always has." His voice cut the air like a dagger.

"I'll say," the secretary said awkwardly, forcing a smile and motioning to walls covered with photographs of mountains he had climbed, of old, iron-adzed ice axes, bights of antique rope, showy commendations from the Italian, British and American Alpine Clubs.

Crutchless, Phil got up and heeled over to an oak bookcase and a silver-framed photograph. He studied the picture for a moment, then wheeled and glared at the secretary. She tilted her head and asked, "Is something wrong?" To her knowledge Phil was a close friend of Harlan's, not a patient.

"Nothing," Phil finally said, "Nothing's wrong." But his voice was all daggers again. Then Harlan arrived.

A svelte, fit man, which his worsted suit was tailored to acknowledge, Harlan's boyish enthusiasm often puzzled patients used to, or at least expecting, a more somber article. But the measured voice and steady green eyes, and most of all the hands, which moved with the lightness of a mime's, let everyone know that Harlan K. Lassiter could be serious enough when need be. The two men talked quietly and about nothing in particular for awhile, for they had not seen one another since Phil's release from the hospital, several weeks before. When Phil had called that morning, his speech fast and tight, Harlan assumed the whole checkered epic had finally caught up with him. Now, seeing how pale and drawn he was, Harlan wondered if he wasn't suffering from a low-grade anemia as well.

A sneak ascent of Chomolari, the last unclimbed, Himalayan mountain, had been Harlan's idea, one he shared with about every other world-class mountaineer who had big plans and the means to pull them off. It was hard to say which was greater: The collective obsession to climb Chomolari, or the universal amazement that it hadn't been climbed already. That there wasn't a single note, article, photo, not one mention of anyone ever even *trying* to climb Chomolari bewildered everyone with a rope and a pair of double-boots. Granted, the Bhutan government had only recently opened the small kingdom to outsiders, and the sacred Chomolari had always been, and still was, "strictly forbidden" to climbers. But it seemed impossible that a few pros had never stolen through Ladahk or Nepal, skirted round the few dozing officials, flashed up the virgin peak and dashed back out—especially given that every other major peak in the region, no matter how grim and remote, now had a route up most every col, face and ridge. With a round trip ticket to Darjeeling, $400 cash and a pair of brass balls, Phil Chambers had finally cleared the air. He'd also barely made it out of the country, and the American ambassador to Bhutan was presently taking so much heat that the state department had revoked Phil's passport. Not that he'd ever need it again. Professional commitments had forced Harlan to pass on the expedition, and he was perfectly astonished that Phil had pushed on anyway, and had pulled it off—alone.

"That's just it!" Phil snapped. "I *wasn't* alone. There were *two* of us."

Harlan had heard some sedated mumbling to this effect just before Phil had left the hospital. Given Phil's condition, he had soft-pedaled around it. Now he owed it to Phil to confront him with the facts and start him down the long dim tunnel toward the light. He grabbed the copy of *Rock & Ice* magazine from his desktop, and read the caption: "Chomolari soloed in nine-day epic." Marveling at the cover photo of the 24,000 foot mountain, Harlan asked, "Have you seen this?" Phil looked down, his eyes lulling unfocused on the rug beneath his bandaged feet.

"We'll work through this together, Phil," Harlan said. "From the beginning."

"Fine," Phil said, "But understand that I did *not* solo Chomolari. There were *two* of us. Me, and Dennis—*your* climbing partner, the person who's been totally forgotten."

Harlan said, "All right. Tell me about the climb."

Phil heaved a sigh at the ceiling: "Well, you know we were first going to try and sneak in through Nepal, but at the last minute Dennis got a trekking permit for Bhutan, so we just went in normal-like. We never mentioned anything about climbing Chomolari, and the few officials who stamped our papers never suspected anything, since there was just the two of us. So we marched away and nobody thought much about us until we got to the monastery just below the mountain. We only camped there for one day, and none of the monks spoke a word of English; but they knew exactly why we were there. The strange thing is that they didn't seem to care about us climbing their sacred mountain, or that we'd get thrown in jail forever if some soldier caught us trying to. They were worried about *us*. And I don't mean about us falling into crevasses or any of that, but about something else, something I wouldn't understand till later."

"What about the actual climb," Harlan asked, trying to get back on track.

"The only thing good was the weather, perfect for eight days. Who's ever heard of that in the Himalayas? Anyway, we took a route up the north face, a steep line, but at least avalanches weren't sweeping down it like everywhere else. The climbing was pretty straightforward early on, but Dennis took a long fall on the second icefield and cut his arm pretty badly; and there were no ledges so we had to hack out platforms in the ice to bivouac, and we froze our asses off because of it. On the sixth day we got to this rotten band of overhanging diorite—but never mind all that. The important thing is that we made the summit on the seventh day.

"We'd probably slept only ten hours in the last week and were trashed. The actual summit was a little rocky bowl we could hunker down in; and we had to because we'd no sooner gotten there than the wind started howling. *Really* howling. I swear the updraft was over 100 miles an hour. Dennis was especially crazy about getting down, along the west rib, which looked easy. His fingers were bad and his arm was swollen but the wind wouldn't let us off. I tell you, Dennis got so desperate to descend he jumped straight off the summit cornice, but the wind just blew him right back up and into the bowl again. We couldn't do anything but pull out all our bivouac gear and put it on. Then the lightning started."

Phil sat on the edge of the chair, twitching slightly. A few beads of perspiration showed on his wan forehead. Harlan said nothing.

"Then the snow came. And hailstones, big as walnuts. A little later the electrical storm got really nasty, with great forks of lightning and thunder that felt like it would shake the mountain apart. Avalanches roared down from all sides. The chill had numbed us half stupid, but we were still there, still plenty aware to realize how bleak things were. Then something, well, something happened. Following this atomic blast of thunder, the winds died off, the snow and hail stopped, and everything went dead still and pitch black. I couldn't see my hand in front of my face. I tried to rise up from the bowl, but my legs wouldn't have it. Some—some *presence* felt to rest on me and weigh me down. And then the bottom seemed to drop out of everything. The normal flow of things had frozen solid. There didn't seem to be a beginning or end to anything. A neverness, sort of. Then the breath of some terrible power blew through me and it felt like I was evaporating—not my body, but *me*—like steam off a kettle. I don't know what the hell was happening, really. I still don't."

Phil clenched his fists, breathing in reedy drafts, trying to pierce the heart of a prodigious mystery. Harlan took it all in soberly, making mental notes throughout.

"Remember," Phil said, "when we'd be swimming out to body surf the big ones at Newport Beach, and a monster would break right in front of us, and how we'd dive down and claw at the bottom of the ocean while a billion tons of wave was tugging at our fins, yanking us toward the beach? Same thing here, but there isn't any wave, and whatever it is, it's sucking my mind right out the top of my head. I can resist, but it's relentless and I'm tired, just like Dennis got tired; and then he was finished. Everything, gone, like he never was."

Harlan wanted to keep Phil going till he'd heard it all, in every detail, so he asked, "About this darkness? How long did it stay like that? An hour? All night?"

"I can't really say," Phil said. "I just remember a blanched sun and the morning. A perfect morning. We could see all the way to Tibet. But we were really spun out and I couldn't feel my toes, so we just bolted down the west rib. By the time we got off late the next day, I could barely walk, and most of Dennis' fingers were black to the first knuckle. Three days later, several of them got gangrenous and I had to carve the tips off with a Swiss Army knife."

"I want you to relax for awhile, Phil," Harlan said. "I'm going to come back in about ten minutes and we'll—"

"No!" Phil said, jumping up and grabbing Harlan's arm. His eyes were like a deer's caught in headlights, and most of the color had drained from his face.

Harlan wanted a few moments alone, to sort through it all, to reference a few sources concerning things completely alien to his normal practice. But Phil was growing increasingly neurotic; plus he was much more than another client, so Harlan decided to stay by him even if it meant more confusion in the short term. He gently eased Phil back into the chair and said, "Phil, believe it. We're going to work through this until we both understand what it's all about."

"It's *about* Dennis!" Phil said bitterly.

"It's about you, Phil," Harlan said. "We can't forget that."

"And we just forget Dennis Pratt?" Phil yelled, "My best friend, the kid you taught how to climb twelve years ago, along with me? Are you saying you've never even heard of the name?!" Phil's eyes were on fire.

When the surgeons had cut off his toes they had amputated Phil's very identity, discarding along with a few lumps of blackened flesh the one thing Phil Chambers was ever any good at, and certainly the only thing he would ever be famous for. Now, he was just a flat-broke nobody who would always walk funny, with a cloudy future and no aspirations. The fires that once drove him were now burning him up, and Harlan knew Phil's hardest climb would be just clawing back onto level ground. He started slowly:

"Phil, what you've been through would have killed a normal man. And losing all your toes doesn't help matters. I want you to understand that the subconscious mind can play tricks on you, can serve up things seemingly as real as the chair you're sitting in. It's all so the individual can survive, can get through something. You're through it, Phil. You've survived. Now—"

"That's just it, Harlan. I *haven't* really survived. And neither did Dennis. None of him. Not so much as a memory. And I'm next."

"Tell me all you can about Dennis," Harlan said, resolved to jump straight into it. Phil didn't move, and his dead voice sounded increasingly weak and distant.

"When we finally left the monastery, we staggered out through Nepal. Once back in the States, it was straight into the hospital. They drugged me silly for the first few days; when I came out of it, I was like this." Phil looked down at his feet, and the little muscles in his jaws flexed.

"Anyway, Dennis was in another wing. Every day cost him another couple fingers, and his kidneys and liver were in a bad way for all the infection. After a week he came around, and was moved into my room. I tell you, the fact that he had two paddles for hands didn't even faze him. Oh, he was terrified all right. But about something else." Phil's voice was so muted now, Harlan had to lean in to hear him.

"He said he felt himself slipping away, sort of shrinking, becoming nothing. Then he started hanging onto everything— bedposts, chairs. It was pitiful, him trying to hold on with those God-awful hands, wrapping his limbs around anything solid, as though something was yanking at him hard. They tried putting him under with Demerol, but that only made things worse. Several days later, he woke me up at maybe three in the morning. He was pale as a corpse. He said he couldn't hold on any longer, that he was compelled to let go to an infinite nothingness that would swallow him whole and forever."

Phil was trembling and twitching horribly. His thin blue veins stood out on his clammy white skin. But heroically, he pressed on.

"I must have nodded off, and when I woke the next morning, an oxygen tent had been pitched next to me and huddled round it were a group of Mexicans. I asked the nurse about it and she said Mr. Fontana was quite ill, worse than the last time *I'd* talked to him. And who's this Mr. Fontana? I'd never talked with any Fontana, had never even *seen* him before then. I questioned everyone and nobody knew a damned thing about Dennis. Once I got released, I went straight to Dennis' house and his folks treated me like a stranger, a lunatic. 'We don't *have* no son,' the old man said. When I tried to force things he told me to back off or he'd call the cops."

Phil stared at Harlan for a moment, his face grim as death; then he glanced over above the oak bookcase, to the silver-framed photograph of Harlan and him on the summit of El Capitan, and grumbled, "Where the hell did you get that picture?"

"Picture?" Harlan asked.

"That El Cap picture. It's doctored!"

"Phil, listen to me. You have got to—"

"No, Harlan. *You've* got to tell *me* why you doctored that photo!"

"The photo has not been doctored, Phil," Harlan said, surprised by the edge in his voice. "Think back, Phil. Think back hard. You set the camera on auto, put it on a rock and we scrambled around in front of it."

"I did not!," Phil yelled.

"It was your camera, Phil," Harlan said with some force.

"It was Dennis' fucking camera!" Phil struggled up on his heels, bracing off the chair and violently waving his free hand at the photo. His face was like putty and white as bone. His hand suddenly fell limp to his side and his voice tapered to a whisper again. "There was three of us on El Cap, Harlan. You, me. . . .and Dennis." And he slouched back into the chair.

Looking at him now, shaking, cadaverous, utterly used up, Harlan wondered if they would ever get to the very bottom of it all. Phil was clearly buckling under something, but Harlan knew it was not some peremptory fist seeking to punch him through the bottom of reality, taking all that he was, had ever been, would ever become. He watched Phil's quaking hand grope for a cigarette.

"Here," Harlan said, grabbing the pack. He handed Phil a smoke, then took one for himself. Harlan lipped his, and walked over to the window. Phil lit his and flicked the matches onto Harlan's desk, landing them next to the issue of *Rock & Ice*.

Harlan wanted to unravel the whole perplexing business so badly he could scream, and that was the problem—letting his own passions muddle his judgement, his objectivity. He recalled the times, some years back, when he and Phil had been pinned down by a whiteout or rock-fall—in the Alps, the Andes, in the Karakorum—and when Phil would start to lose it he would grab him by the shoulders and say, "Deal with the fear, Phil, or it will deal with you." Now he again wanted to grab Phil by the shoulders and say— He didn't know what. Those days of seeing them both through a pinch were long past. Phil had gotten world-class and could, and did, deal with anything. He'd soloed Chomolari for Christ's sakes.

I'm too close to all this, Harlan thought. I'm going to need some help breaking through. Hamstrung, he gazed through the window at the chugging busses and shuddering palms and their starkness momen-tarily absorbed him. He blinked twice, and a little shiver moved through him. Then he turned and looked for a match, spotting a book on his desk. He lit his smoke and waved out the flame, noting the words on the match cover: "Nothing is forgotten, just forgiven." Always the same childish rot from these evangelists, Harlan chuckled to himself, trouser-ing the matches. But that's no kid stuff, he thought, picking up the *Rock & Ice* to admire the magnificent and "unclimbed" Chomolari. Like so many other top climbers, it baffled him how such an obvious prize should remain virgin. Sure, the sacred Chomolari was strictly off limits to climbers, but to a world-class talent like Harlan K. Lassiter, there were always ways around silly regulations. He knew—had vowed to himself, actually—that he would be first, that this coming summer he would finally get to Bhutan and bag Chomolari, last of the unclimbed Himalayan peaks. Yes, he was that good. Whenever he doubted it, which he rarely did, he'd walk over to the silver-framed photograph above the oak bookcase and study his photograph atop El Capitan—after his solo ascent. A buzzer sounded and a breathy voice intoned:

"Mrs. Goldfarb is here to see you, Doctor."

"I'll be with her in a couple minutes," Harlan said, butting his smoke and scrambling to prepare for the afternoon patients.

SUMMARY:

1. Phil Chambers, recently returned from an expedition in which he ascended the previously unclimbed Chomolari, rides a bus to the office of his psychiatrist-friend Harlan Lassiter.

2. Phil is weak, frost-bitten and emotionally distraught. He feels an alien force pulling at him, which he hopes Harlan can help him overcome. In the meantime, he uses breathing taught to him by monks in Bhutan while he and his buddy, Dennis, recovered from the climb.

3. Harlan's office holds photos of climbing expeditions the two have gone on. He marvels at Phil's accomplishment—conquering Chomolari solo.

4. Phil retorts he didn't climb the peak alone. He explains there were two on the climb—himself and Dennis, a former climbing partner of Harlan's.

5. Phil and Dennis snuck into Bhutan. They were surprised that the monks in the monastery at the mountain's foot weren't concerned about their

climbing the forbidden mountain, but were inexplicably worried about the two climbers.

6. The climbers had fine weather for the seven-day ascent. But once on top, the weather became violent—a vicious thunderstorm sent avalanches down all faces of the mountain and pinned the two on the summit. Suddenly, the storm abated and everything went black. A presence began to suck at them, drawing on their very souls.

7. They made an epic descent of the peak—Dennis lost his fingers to frostbite. Harlan reminds Phil this is about him, but Phil insists it's about Dennis: "We just can't forget him."

8. Once back in the state, Phil and Dennis went to the same hospital to recuperate. Dennis was in bad shape, but not just physically. Dennis said something was yanking at him; that he was being pulled into an infinite nothingness. The next day, when Phil woke up, Dennis was gone—another man was in his bed—and no one, not even his parents, seemed to know who he was.

9. As he tells the story, Harlan notices Phil seems to be getting more translucent, more distracted. Phil points to a picture of him and Harlan on the top of Yosemite's El Capitan, asking why it has been doctored—Dennis should be in it. Harlan insists no one but the two of them were on the climb.

10. While trying to reconcile Phil's problem, Harlan turns his back and muses, thinking about various climbs with Phil and without him.

11. When he turns back, he picks up a copy of a climbing magazine, which features on its cover the

magnificent unclimbed Chomolari. He glances at a photo he took of himself after his solo ascent of El Capitan, and decides he should attempt a solo climb of the mysterious peak.

ANNABEL LEE

by Edgar Allan Poe

It was many and many a year ago,
    In a kingdom by the sea,
That a maiden there lived whom you may know
    By the name of Annabel Lee;
And this maiden she lived with no other thought
    Than to love and be loved by me.

I was a child and *she* was a child,
    In this kingdom by the sea:
But we loved with a love that was more than love—
    I and Annabel Lee;
With a love that the winged seraphs of heaven
    Coveted her and me.

And this was the reason that, long ago,
    In the kingdom by the sea,
A wind blew out of a cloud, chilling
    My beautiful Annabel Lee;
So that her highbrow kinsman came
    And bore her away from me,
To shut her up in a sepulchre
    In this kingdom by the sea.

The angels, not half so happy in heaven,
    Went envying her and me—
Yes!—that was the reason (as all men know,
    in this kingdom by the sea)
That the wind came out of the cloud by night,
    Chilling and killing my Annabel Lee.
But our love it was stronger by far than the love
    Of those who were older than we—
    Of many far wiser than we—

And neither the angels in heaven above,
    Nor the demons down under the sea,
Can ever dissever my soul from the soul
    Of the beautiful Annabel Lee.
For the moon never beams, without bringing me dreams
    Of the beautiful Annabel Lee;

And the stars never rise, but I feel the bright eyes
    Of the beautiful Annabel Lee;
And so, all the night-tide, I lie down by the side
Of my darling—my darling—my life and my bride,
    In the sepulchre there by the sea,
    In her tomb by the sounding sea.

QUITE DISCOURAGED AND IMPATIENT FOR HIS DEATH

by George Yount

Movies and popular fiction show us that mountain men were tough hombres. How about reality? Here's an account from the memoirs of fur trapper George Yount of how a fellow trapper, named Hugh Glass, mangled by a grizzly bear and left to die, walked 300 miles to postpone that fate.

Among the numerous veteran Trappers, with whom Yount became acquainted, and was from time to time associated, was one by the name of Glass. In point of adventure, dangers and narrow escapes, and capacity for endurance and the sufferings which befell him, this man was preeminent. He was bold, daring, reckless and eccentric to a high degree; but was nevertheless a man of great talents and intellectual as well as bodily power. But his bravery was conspicuous beyond all his other qualities for the perilous life he led.

With the Pawnees, Glass roamed the wilderness in security many months, until they visited St. Louis, where he found means to escape from the Indians. Having resided in the City some eight or ten months, Ashley sought him out and employed him to join a band of Thirty Trappers, which he had furnished and equipped to trap upon the Yellow Stone River under Major Henry.

Glass, with this party of Trappers, ascended the Missouri, till they reached the territory of the Pickarees (Arickara).

Glass, as was usual, could not be kept in obedience to orders with the band, but perservered to thread his way alone through the bushes and chaparral. As the hunters were wending their way up the River, a man named Allen spotted Glass dodging along in the forest alone, and said to his companion, "There, look at that fellow, Glass; see him foolishly exposing his life. I wish some Grizzly Bear would pounce upon him and teach him a lesson of obedience to orders, and to keep in his place. He is ever off, scouting in the bushes and exposing his life and himself to dangers."

Glass disappeared in the chaparral, and within half an hour his screams were heard. The two hunters hastened to his relief and discovered a huge Grizzly Bear, with two Cubs. The monster had seized Glass, torn the flesh from the lower part of the body, and from the lower limbs. He also had his neck shockingly torn, even to the degree that an aperture appeared to have been made in the windpipe, and his breath to exude at the side of his neck. Blood flowed freely, but fortunately no bone was broken, and his hands and arms were not disabled.

The whole party was soon there, the monster and her cubs were slain, and the victim cared for in the best degree possible, under existing circumstances. A convenient hand litter was prepared and the sufferer carried by his humane fellow trappers from day to day. He retained all his faculties but those of speech and locomotion. Too feeble to walk, or help himself at all, his comrades every moment waited for his death. Day by day they ministered to his wants and no one counted it any hardship.

Among those rude and rough trappers of the wilderness, fellow feeling and devotion to each other's wants is a remarkable and universal feature or characteristic. It is admirable and worthy the imitation of even the highest grade of civilized men. We have remarked it at every step in the investigation, which, in preparing this work, has devolved on us.

After having thus carried Glass during six days, it became necessary for the party to hasten their journey, as the season for trapping was fast transpiring. Major Henry therefore offered four hundred Dollars to any two of his men who would volunteer to remain until he should die, decently bury him and then press on their way to overtake the main body. One man and boy volunteered to remain. They did so, and the party urged forward towards the Yellow Stones.

The two waited several days, and he still lived. No change was apparent. They dressed his wounds daily, and fed and nourished him with water from the spring and such light food as he could swallow. Still he was speechless but could use his hands. Both his lower limbs were quite disabled. As he lay by the spring, Buffalo berries hung in clusters and in great profusion over him and around his bed, which was made soft with dry leaves and two blankets.

Quite discouraged and impatient for his death, as there remained no hope of his recovery, the two resolved to leave him there to die alone in the wilderness. They took from him his knife, camp kettle and Rifle, laid him smoothly on his blankets, and left him thus to die a lingering death, or be torn in pieces by ferocious wild beasts and to be seen no more till they should meet him at the dread tribunal of eternal judgement.

He could hear their every word, but could not speak nor move his body. His arms he could use, and he stretched them out imploringly, but in vain. They departed and silence reigned around him. Oppressed with grief and his hard fate, he soon became delirious. Visions of benevolent beings appeared. Around him were numerous friendly faces, smiling encouragement and exhorting him not to despond, and assuring him that all would be well at last. He declared to Yount that he was never alone, by day or by night.

He could reach the water and take it to mouth in the hollow of his hand, and could pluck the berries from the bushes to eat as he might need. One morning, after several weeks, he found by his side a huge Rattlesnake. With a small stone he slew the reptile, jambed off its head and cast it from him. Having laid the dead serpant by his side he jambed off small parts from time to time, and bruised it thoroughly and moistened it with water from the spring and made it a grateful food on which he fed from day to day.

At length the wolves came and took from under him his blankets, and having dragged them some distance, tore them in pieces. Thus he was left solely on his bed of leaves. In this condition he must have lain many weeks, how many he could never tell.

Meantime the two, the man and boy, false to their trust, came up with Major Henry and the party, and reported that Glass had died and they had decently buried his remains, and brought his effects with them, his gun, his knife and camp kettle, and received the promised reward for their fidelity—four hundred Dollars.

After a long period, his strength began to revive, and he crawled a few rods, and laid himself down again during several days. Then again he resumed his journey, every day increasing his distance some rods.

After many long and tedious days, and even weeks, he found himself upon his feet and began to walk. Soon he could travel nearly a mile in a day. This distance he increased daily more and more. Thus covered with wounds, which would frequently bleed, and require much attention, he urged his journey through a howling wilderness. Often by the way he would find the decaying carcasses of buffaloes, which, wounded by the hunter, or some more powerful animal, had died. From these he gained nourishing food, by pounding out the marrow from the bones and eating it seasoned with buffalo-berries and moistened with limpid water from the brooks and springs. With sharp stones he would dig from the earth nourishing roots, which he had learned to discriminate while sojourning with the Pawnees.

After many weeks and a distance of more than two hundred miles, he reached the nearest trading post (Fort Kiowa), and passed the winter, as Autumn had worn away, and the cold season had overtaken him there. During the bracing season of winter, his strength was rapidly restored. As the following spring opened (actually in October), he found himself again a well man, and able to resume his journey to rejoin Major Henry and his band of trappers. Fortunately as he was about to depart, an express party arrived, on its way to carry orders to Major Henry, at his post in Yellow Stone, and Glass joined this party (under Antoine Langevin) to accompany them to Henry's Fort.

SUMMARY:

1. A trapper named Glass was traveling with other trappers in the Old West when he was attacked and viciously mauled by a grizzly bear.

2. His companions cared for his seemingly life-threatening wounds, carrying them with him on a litter. But finally, as the trapping season grew to a close, it was decided that Glass, who was unable to move or speak, would have to be left behind.

3. The leader of the trappers assigned two men to stay with Glass until he died, then to rejoin the group, offering to pay the two four-hundred dol-

lars. The man and boy stayed with Glass for two days; the latter had use of his hands and arms, but his lower limbs were mangled, and it was clear he wouldn't live. Impatient, the two decided to abandon him, leaving him beside a stream on a buffalo pelt to die alone.

4. Glass found himself alone, but unwilling to succumb. He drank water he scooped with his hands from the stream and ate berries from nearby bushes. He awoke one morning to find a huge rattlesnake beside him; he slew the snake with a stone, and feasted on the meat.

5. While the two who had abandoned him received their reward, Glass gradually regained his strength. He found himself able to crawl a bit, and slowly that distance grew longer, until he was able to drag himself a mile a day.

6. As he crept along, he fed on carcasses and whatever else he could find. Finally, he reached Fort Kiowa, where he recuperated. The next year, he was able to rejoin the same trapping party that had abandoned him the year before.

A Horseman in the Sky

by Ambrose Bierce

One sunny afternoon in the autumn of 1861 a soldier lay in a clump of laurel by the side of a road in western Virginia. He lay at full length upon his stomach, his extended right hand loosely grasping his rifle. But for the slight rhythmic movement of the cartridge-box at the back of his belt he might have been thought to be dead. He was asleep at his post. But if detected he would be dead shortly afterward, death being the just and legal penalty of his crime.

The clump of laurel in which the criminal lay was in the angle of a road which after ascending southward a steep acclivity to that point turned sharply to the west, running along the summit for perhaps one hundred yards. There it turned southward again and went zigzagging downward through the forest. At the salient of that second angle was a large flat rock, jutting out northward, overlooking the deep valley from which the road ascended. The rock capped a high cliff: a stone dropped from its edge would have fallen sheer downward one thousand feet to the tops of the pines. The angle where the soldier lay was on another spur of the same cliff. Had he been awake he would have commanded a view, not only of the short arm of the road and the jutting rock, but of the entire profile of the cliff below it.

The country was wooded everywhere except at the bottom of the valley to the northward, where there was a small natural meadow through which flowed a stream scarcely visible from the valley's rim. This open ground looked hardly larger than an ordinary door-yard, but was really several acres in extent. Its green was more vivid than that of the inclosing forest. Away beyond it rose a line of giant cliffs similar to those upon which we are supposed to stand in our survey of the savage scene, and through which the road had somehow made its climb to the summit. The configuration of the valley, indeed, was such that from this point of observation it seemed entirely shut in, and one could but have wondered how the road which found a way out of it had found a way into it, and whence came and whither went the waters of the stream that parted the meadow more than a thousand feet below.

No country is so wild and difficult but men will make it a theatre of war. Concealed in the forest at the bottom of that military rat-trap, in which half a hundred men in possession of the exits might have starved an army to submission, lay five regiments of Federal infantry. They had marched all the previous day and night and were resting. At nightfall they would take to the road again, climb to the place where their sentinel now slept, and descending the other slope of the ridge fall upon a camp of the enemy at about midnight. Their hope was to surprise it, for the road led to the rear of it. In case of failure, their position would be perilous, and fail they surely would should accident or vigilance apprise the enemy of the movement.

The sleeping sentinel was a young Virginian named Carter Druse. He was the son of wealthy parents, an only child, and had known such ease and cultivation and high living as wealth and taste were able to command in the mountain country of western Virginia. His home was but a few miles from where he now lay. One morning he had risen from the breakfast-table and said, quietly but gravely: "Father, a Union regiment has arrived at Grafton. I am going to join it."

The father lifted his leonine head, looked at the son a moment in silence, and replied: "Well, go, sir, and whatever may occur do what you conceive to be your duty. Virginia, to which you are a traitor, must get on without you. Should we both live to the end of the war, we will speak further of the matter. Your mother, as the physician has informed you, is in a most critical condition; at the best she cannot be with us longer than a few weeks, but that time is precious. It would be better not to disturb her."

So Carter Druse, bowing reverently to his father, who returned the salute with a stately courtesy that masked a breaking heart, left the home of his childhood to go soldiering. By conscience and courage, he soon commended himself to his fellows and his officers; and it was to these qualities and to some knowledge of the country that he owed his selection for his present perilous duty at the extreme outpost. Nevertheless, fatigue had been stronger than resolution and he had fallen asleep. What good or bad angel came in a dream to rouse him from his state of crime, who shall say? Without a movement, without a sound, in the profound silence and the languor of the late afternoon, some invisible messenger of fate whispered into his spirit the mysterious awakening word which no human lips ever have spoken, no human memory ever has recalled. He quietly raised his forehead from his arm and looked between the masking stems of the laurels, instinctively closing his right hand about the stock of his rifle.

His first feeling was a keen artistic delight. On a colossal pedestal, the cliff—motionless at the extreme edge of the capping rock and sharply outlined against the sky—was an equestrian statue of impressive dignity. The figure of the man sat on the figure of the horse, straight and soldierly, but with the repose of a Grecian god carved in marble. The gray costume harmonized with its aerial background; the metal of accoutrement and comparison was softened by the shadow; the animal's skin had no points of high light. A carbine strikingly foreshortened lay across the pommel of the saddle, kept in place by the right hand grasping it at the "grip." In silhouette against the sky the profile of the horse was cut with the sharpness of a cameo, gazing across the heights of air to the confronting cliffs beyond. The face of the rider, turned slightly away, showed only an outline of temple and beard; he was looking downward to the bottom of the valley. Magnified by its lift against the sky and by the soldier's testifying sense of the formidableness of a near enemy the group appeared of heroic, almost colossal, size.

For an instant Druse had a strange, half-defined feeling that he had slept to the end of the war and was looking upon a noble work of art reared upon that eminence to commemorate the deeds of an heroic past of which he had been a inglorious part. The feeling was dispelled by a slight movement of the group: the horse, without moving its feet, had drawn its body slightly backward from the verge. The man remained immobile as before. Broad awake and keenly alive to the significance of the situation, Druse now brought the butt of his rifle against his cheek by cautiously pushing the barrel forward through the bushes, cocked the piece, and glancing through the sights covered a vital spot of the horseman's breast. A touch upon the trigger and all would have been well with Carter Druse. At that instant the horseman turned his head and looked in the direction of his concealed foeman—seemed to look into his very face, into his eyes, into his brave, compassionate heart.

It is then so terrible to kill an enemy in war—an enemy who has surprised a secret vital to the safety of one's self and comrades—an enemy more formidable for his knowledge than all his army for its numbers. Carter Druse grew pale; he shook in every limb, turned faint, and saw the statuesque group before him as black figures, rising, falling, moving unsteadily in arcs of circles in a fiery sky. His hand fell away from his weapon, his head slowly dropped until his face rested on the leaves in which he lay. This courageous gentleman and hardy soldier was near swooning from emotion.

It was not for long. In another moment his face was raised from earth, his hands resumed their places on the rifle, his forefinger sought the trigger; mind, heart, and eyes were clear, conscience and reason sound. He could not hope to capture that enemy; to alarm him would but send him dashing to his camp with his fatal news. The duty of the soldier was plain: the man must be shot dead from ambush—without warning, without a moment's spiritual preparation, with never so much as an unspoken prayer, he must be sent to his account. But no—there is a hope; he may have discovered nothing—perhaps he is but admiring the sublimity of the landscape. If permitted, he may turn and ride carelessly away in the direction whence he came. Surely it will be possible to judge at the instant of his withdrawing whether he knows. It may well be that his fixity of attention—Druse turned his head and looked through the deeps of air downward, as from the surface to the bottom of a translucent sea. He saw creeping across the green meadow a sinuous line of figures of men and horses—some foolish commander was permitting the soldiers of his escort to water their beasts in the open, in plain view from a dozen summits!

Druse withdrew his eyes from the valley and fixed them again upon the man and horse in the sky, and again it was through the sights of his rifle. But this time his aim was at the horse. In his memory, as if they were a divine mandate, rang the words of his father at their parting: "Whatever may occur, do what you conceive to be your duty." He was calm now. His teeth were firmly closed; his nerves were as tranquil as a sleeping babe's; his breathing, until suspended in the act of taking aim, was regular and slow. Duty had conquered; the spirit had said to the body: "Peace, be still." He fired.

A Horseman in the Sky

An officer of the Federal force, who in a spirit of adventure or in quest of knowledge had left the hidden bivouac in the valley, and with aimless feet had made his way to the lower edge of a small open space near the foot of the cliff, was considering what he had to gain by pushing his exploration further. At a distance of a quarter-mile before him, but apparently at a stone's throw, rose from its fringe of pines the gigantic face of rock, towering to so great a height above him that it made him giddy to look up to where its edge cut a sharp, rugged line against the sky. It presented a clean, vertical profile against a background of blue sky to a point half the way down, and of distant hills, hardly less blue, thence to the tops of the trees at its base. Lifting his eyes to the dizzy altitude of its summit the officer saw an astonishing sight—a man on horseback riding down into the valley through the air!

Straight upright sat the rider, in military fashion, with a firm seat in the saddle, a strong clutch upon the rein to hold his charger from too impetuous a plunge. From his bare head his long hair streamed upward, waving like a plume. His hands were concealed in the cloud of the horse's lifted mane. The animal's body was as level as if every hoofstroke encountered the resistant earth. Its motions were those of a wild gallop, but even as the officer looked they ceased, with all the legs thrown sharply forward as in the act of alighting from a leap. But this was a flight!

Filled with amazement and terror by this apparition of a horseman in the sky—half believing himself the chosen scribe of some new Apocalypse, the officer was overcome by the intensity of his emotions; his legs failed him and he fell. Almost the same instant he heard a crashing sound in the trees—a sound that died without an echo—and all was still.

The officer rose to his feet, trembling. The familiar sensation of an abraded shin recalled his dazed faculties. Pulling himself together he ran rapidly away from the cliff to a point distant from its foot; thereabout he expected to find his man; and thereabout he naturally failed. In the fleeting instant of his vision his imagination had been so wrought upon by the apparent grace and ease and intention of the marvelous performance that it did not occur to him that the line of march of aerial cavalry is directly downward, and that he could find the objects of his search at the very foot of the cliff. A half-hour later he returned to camp.

This officer was a wise man; he knew better than to tell an incredible truth. He had said nothing of what he had seen. But when the commander asked him if in his scout he had learned anything of advantage to the expedition, he answered:

"Yes, sir; there is no road leading down into the valley from the southward."

The commander, knowing better, smiled.

After firing his shot, Private Carter Druse reloaded his rifle and resumed his watch. Ten minutes had hardly passed when a Federal sergeant crept cautiously to him on hands and knees. Druse neither turned his head nor looked at him, but lay without motion or sign of recognition.

"Did you fire?" the sergeant whispered.

"Yes."

"At what?"

"A horse. It was standing on yonder rock—pretty far out. It went over the cliff."

The man's face was white, but he showed no other sign of emotion. Having answered, he turned away his eyes and said no more. The sergeant did not understand.

"See here, Druse," he said, after a moment's silence, "it's no use making a mystery. Was there anybody on the horse?"

"Yes."

"Well?"

"My father."

SUMMARY:

1. A soldier dozed while on sentry. His station was on a point far above a wooded valley; he slept concealed beneath bushes.

2. Below, factions of both the Union and Confederate army sought each other out to engage in battle.

3. The sentry was the son of wealthy Virginians. When he had joined the Union regiment, his father had declared him a traitor to Virgina, but said

should they both survive the war, they would speak of it then.

4. Something benevolent caused him to awake. From his hiding place in the laurel, he spied a man on a horse, straight and soldierly, wearing the gray uniform of the enemy. The horseman looked down from the point toward the valley where the young soldier, called Druse, knew his regiment was marching.

5. Suddenly, the horseman turned toward Druse's hiding place, and the soldier grew pale, knowing he would have to kill the courageous gentleman, whose brave, compassionate heart he could see in his face. He first put the man in his rifle sight, then leveled his sight on the horse. As he fired, he heard the words of his father, "Whatever may occur, do what you conceive to be your duty."

6. Below, an officer of the Federal forces witnesses an astonishing sight—a man on horseback riding down into the valley through the air. He was astonished at the aristocratic style of the horse and its rider, until the two crashed into the trees near him.

7. Later, a Federal man crept up to Druse, who remained at his post. "Did you fire?" he asked. Druse replied yes, that he had fired at a horse. "Was there anybody on the horse?" the soldier asked. "My father," Druse replied.

THE GREAT SPHINX

The Great Sphinx has a woman's head and breasts, the wings of a bird, and the body and feet of a lion. Some give it the body of a dog and a snake's tail. It is told that it depopulated the Thebaine countryside asking riddles (for it had a human voice) and making a meal of any man who could not give the answer. Of Oedipus, the son of Jocasta, the Sphinx asked, "What has four legs, two legs, and three legs, and the more legs it has the weaker it is?" Oedipus answered that it was a man who as an infant crawls on all fours, when he grows up walks on two legs, and in old age leans on a staff. The riddle solved, the Sphinx threw herself from a precipice.

From Jorge Luis Borges' *The Book of Imaginary Beings*

LUCERO

by Oscar Castro Z.

Outlined one against the other, the crests of the mountain chain seemed shuffled like a deck of stony cards as far as Ruben Olmos' eyes could see. Dazzling white peaks, bluish draws, upjutting minarets rose before his gaze, rising and falling in the harsh light, more inaccessible as the rider mounted on. Before starting up an abrupt and tiring gulch, he gave a rest to his horse, which was panting like bellows. Crossing a leg over the saddle, his eyes wandered down to the mirror-like glimmer of the river winding through pastures and maize fields. Then, his view shifted beyond plats of trodden red earth inside several corrals, and sought the drowsy pueblo he had left that morning. There it was framed in the distance, the houses like toys in a shop window, and the dim ravines of its streets. The reflections of a few zinc plate roofs darted back the sun's brilliance, cutting the air with blinding silver streaks.

With a flutter of his eyelids Ruben Olmos rubbed out the picture of the valley and examined his mount, whose damp flanks rose and fell in labored rhythm.

"You're getting old, Lucero," he said affectionately. As if he understood, the animal turned its face toward him, a black face with a white star on its forehead. Ruben had a deeper tie with Lucero than with human beings. It must have been because the horse did not answer, or because he always said "Yes" with his moist eyes. There was no telling.

"Well, it's a sure thing that you have worked plenty, but you have many years of travel ahead of you yet. At least, while there are still some mountains around here."

He turned to gaze at the Andes, fierce yet familiar; for thirteen years they had crossed and recrossed this great cordillera. Dazed by the white blaze of the sun on the snow, Ruben thought of his friends and of the lead they had over him. Significant, but he did not worry, certain as he was he and Lucero would overtake them before nightfall.

"So long as you go along with me, we won't have to spend the night alone," he declared to his horse.

Ruben Olmos was born with flesh fashioned out of hard substance. His coppery skin and flattened nose bespoke Indian blood, and his smile, dimmed by dark eyes, only occasionally gleamed at the edge of his teeth. He gave the impression of self- confidence, but little else. A herdsman amidst solitudes, he had learned from them silence and penetration. On horseback he was always the leader, not one to be led. As this energy needed space to find play, nowhere seemed more favorable to his talents and passions than the tumultuous heights of the Andes.

He had learned his difficult art from his father, who had taken him even as a child over the precipices and through ravines in spite of his unwillingness and the fear that the mountains at first had roused in him. When the old man died, peacefully in his bed, the ranch owner appointed Ruben, then seventeen, as successor. He had crossed hundreds of times this mountain barrier which, in his younger days, had seemed to him impassible, leading numerous herds of cattle to Cuyo, always with fortune on his side.

He chose Lucero when the animal was still a frisking colt, and had broken him in himself. The rider had never been willing to use another mount, although his boss had presented him with two other horses apparently more powerful and from better stock. Lucero had become a partner with whom he traveled with a sort of superstition induced by hazardous life. If some day he were asked to choose between losing his brother and losing Lucero, he would hesitate before making up his mind because this creature, more than a mere conveyance, inspired in him from the beginning the feeling of a friend. More than a friend. It seemed as if the push of his muscles flowed into the tendons of Lucero.

"We must be moving, old man."

Setting his iron shoes into the cracks, the horse ascended toward heaven. The rider, bent forward, moved with the rhythmic sway of each step. Pebbles rolled down into the depths and the rings on the reins tinkled. And Lucero—toc, toc, toc—was finally there on the crest after toiling upwards for a quarter-hour.

Upon the heights the wind glided over the rider's face, bearing more cold and moisture. It sought some opening in his cloak, but long practice made Ruben safe from its attack. The loneliness on this roof of the world was so immense, so desolate that some travelers had the swift sensation of drowning in the wind, as if they were swirling in the depths of treacherous waters. The wind blast persisted, but it could not alter Ruben Olmos' course.

With several crests of the mountains crossed, the valley he'd left was no longer visible. Ahead were great mountain walls, toward which the eye was drawn. And above stretched a thin sky, pure, bluer than the wind, hardly speckled by the flashing arc of an eagle, king of air and solitudes. But Ruben did not have time to admire the magnificent spans of the landscape. The deep orchestral tones of the verdure, the symphony of birds and insects which mounted upward in delicate surges—none of these found an echo in his spirit, forged as it was out of the dark materials of struggle and decision.

From a rise that gave a clear view of the nearby peaks, Ruben Olmos scanned the path in the hope of seeing those who had gone before him. But he perceived nothing but emptiness ahead. The rider pursed his lips. The four companions who had left the ranch an hour ahead of him had gained quite a lead. He would have to press his horse.

On he went past the familiar landmarks: The Lion's Cave, the Condor's Perch, the Black Gap. "My friends must be waiting for me in the Muleteer's Shelter," he thought, and sank his spurs into Lucero's ribs.

The path was little more than a vague track from whose line eyes less experienced than his might stray. But the slight rut over which he traveled was, for Ruben Olmos, a wide and spacious thoroughfare leading to one goal: The pueblo of Cuyo.

As he gained higher terrain, hawthorn, rosemary and stunted cactus, crooked by the storms, lay up like dark splashes from a painter's brush against the pale snow. The solitudes grew whiter and deeper. Ruben imagined it was five o'clock in the afternoon. The sun, already slipping into the west, struggled to sift its warmth through the wind.

Suddenly, they emerged into an immense stadium of stone. Two towering mountains framed it, each with its vertical cliffside girding a crevice whose depths could not be plumbed. It looked as though an immense cataclysm had severed the mountain chain at a blow.

Ruben Olmos reined in Lucero. This, the Vulture Pass, exerted a strange fascination on his mind. When he was fifteen and had crossed it for the first time, on a whim and despite his father's warning, he had looked down into the dark chasm: after a moment the yawning void seemed to whirl around like a blue funnel. Something like an invisible claw was pulling him into it and he was letting himself go. "Turn your head around, you fool!" his father shouted, observing the danger. From that time on, in spite of all his calm control, he had not dared let his gaze wander into that unfathomable depth.

The Vulture's Pass had its legends. No herd of cattle could cross it on Good Friday without suffering some terrible misfortune. His father had been the first to tell him so, citing well-established accounts of cattle and horses being swallowed up in some mysterious way by the abyss. It was also known that, over the ages, numerous drovers had been drawn into the hungry maw for stealing from the church, or cheating on their wives; on Ash Wednesday, the echoes of their anguished cries swirled up with the winds.

In fact, this pass was one of the most impressive in the entire Andes. The path—merely a slender stone shelf—was barely three-feet wide, just enough to let an animal traverse between the stone wall on the left and the sheer drop on the right.

Before venturing across, Ruben Olmos complied scrupulously with the covenant established generations ago by those who crossed these mountains: He drew his pistol from its holster and fired a shot into the air to give warning to any possible traveler that the route was occupied and he was to wait. The explosion sent out a shock wave that volleyed through the close, vertical mountains, thundering up and finally out into the blue expanse a half-mile above. After a short pause, the rider started across. Lucero, carefully setting his iron shoes on the rocky shelf, was apparently unaware of any change in the nature of the route. "Splendid horse," mused the rider, summing up all his veneration for the animal.

Upon emerging from an abrupt turn, Ruben Olmos' heart gave one wild leap in his breast. From the opposite direction, less than twenty paces away, appeared a man mounted on a dark sorrel-colored nag. Amazement, frustration and anger flashed across the faces of the riders.

Both, with an instinctive pull, reined in their horses. The first to break the anguished silence was the man on the sorrel. After a growling curse, he shouted, "And how did you ever presume to start on this way without giving warning?"

Ruben Olmos knew that mere words would not help. He kept on advancing till the heads of the two horses almost touched. Then, in a quiet firm voice that seemed to come from deep in his chest, he said, "It was you, my friend, who didn't give the signal shot."

The other drew his revolver and Ruben did likewise, with a promptness unsuspected in him. They looked at each other fixedly for a moment, with a spark of defiance in their eyes. The stranger had whetted grey eyes and features that betrayed inner steel and decisiveness. His aspect and assurance revealed he was a mountaineer accustomed to danger. Both realized that they were worthy adversaries. Pointing his weapon into the abyss, so as not to arouse mistrust, Ruben Olmos drew out the empty cartridge and presented it to the stranger, saying, "Here is my shot."

The stranger did the same, likewise offering as proof a leadless shell.

The two men stared dismayed at the other's spent cartridge, as much proof of their word as of the dreadful decision awaiting them. "Tough luck, my friend," the stranger finally said. "We fired at the same time."

"That's how it was, friend," said Ruben Olmos. "And now what are we going to do?"

"As for going back, it just can't be done."

"Agreed."

"One of us will have to go along on foot."

"Yes, that is so. But which one of us?"

"Luck will have to decide that."

And without another comment the sorrel rider took a coin from his pocket and put it between his hands without looking.

"You say which," he said.

There was a terrible hesitation in Ruben's mind. Those two clamped hands hid the secret of a merciless verdict. Destiny would speak through them in an impartial voice more inexorable and final than all the courts of man. But as Ruben Olmos never defied the decrees of uncertain fate, he pronounced the word that someone whispered in his brain:

"Heads."

The stranger slowly uncovered the coin and the oblique afternoon sun lit up a laurel wreath circling a rearing stallion, a cornucopia and a scroll.

Ruben Olmos had lost.

He did not betray by the slightest gesture his inner dismay. His eyes turned softly and slowly toward the head and neck of Lucero. Presently, his hand gestured the caress that burst from his heart. And finally, as if to free himself from the task bearing down on him, he let himself drop to the path over the shining croup of his horse. He untied the rifle and the provision-bag attached to the saddle. Then he slipped off the blanket roll resting on the animal's haunch. And all this slowly created between the two men a silence more dreadful than the Andean solitude.

During these preparations the stranger seemed to suffer as much as the loser. Pretending to see nothing, he anxiously braided and unbraided the thongs of his whip. Ruben Olmos was deeply grateful for this feigned indifference. When his work was done, he said to the other in a voice of desperate firmness, "Did you happen to meet four herdsmen with two mules on the way?"

"Yes, they're resting at the Refuge. Are they your companions?"

"Yes, it happens they are."

Lucero, perhaps surprised to be free from the saddle in such an unlikely spot, turned his head, and Ruben gazed for a moment upon his eyes, gentle as dark pools. The star on his forehead. His ears erect. His nostrils quivering.

"Keep a close rein on your beast, friend," Ruben said.

The other pulled in the reins, turning the head of his sorrel toward the rocky wall.

Only then did Ruben Olmos, his heart dissolved in agony, lightly pat Lucero's neck once more, and with an immense shove send him plunging into the abyss.

SUMMARY:

1. Ruben Olmos rides his old, faithful horse, Lucero, out of his village toward the Andes. Lucero, he muses, is his best friend, for he always says yes, and he always was there.

2. Olmos and Lucero have herded cattle through the ravines and over the precipices of the Andes from the sea to the jungle for 13 years. Together they had weathered many dangers and to Ruben, it seemed their muscles moved together.

3. On this day, the two were climbing the heights to catch up with those who had gone before. As Ruben scanned the heights, he saw familiar sights—The Lion's Cave, the Condor's Perch, the Black Gap. His friends, he figured, were waiting for him at the Muleteer's Shelter.

4. Rider and horse climbed on, until they came to a great stadium of stone. This was Vulture Pass, and could only be traversed on a path that was wide enough only for a single horseman. Legend told of the powers of the pass, which could lure the unwary into the chasm below the shelf.

5. Olmos followed the tradition established years before—he fired his pistol once, to warn anyone on the other side of the pass that the route was occupied.

6. Olmos and Lucero were halfway across, however, when they encountered another rider on a sorrel nag. The two were incredulous, accusing each other of not firing a warning shot. But they found they both had spent shells, and realized they had fired at the same time.

7. Since there was no way to pass, and no way to turn around, the two decided one would have to proceed on foot. The stranger took a coin from his pocket, and Olmos called heads. It was tails.

8. Slowly, lovingly, Olmos dismounted Lucero; he patted his neck one more time, then pushed him into the abyss.

BRIDGE OF SIGHS

by Thomas Hood

One more unfortunate,
Weary of breath,
Rashly importunate,
Gone to her death!

Take her up tenderly,
Lift her with care;
Fashioned so slenderly,
Young, and so fair!

Look at her garments
Clinging like cerements;
Whilst the wave constantly
Drips from her clothing;
Take her up instantly,
Loving, not loathing.

Touch her not scornfully;
Think of her mournfully,
Gently and humanly;
Not of the stains of her,
All that remains of her
Now, is pure womanly.

Make no deep scrutiny
Into her mutiny
Rash and undutiful:
Past all dishonor,
Death has left on her
Only the beautiful.

Still, for all slips of hers,
One of Eve's family—
Wipe those poor lips of hers
Oozing so clammily.

Thomas Hood

Loop up her tresses
Escaped from the comb,
Her fair auburn tresses;
Whilst wonderment guesses
Where was her home?

Who was her father?
Who was her mother?
Had she a sister?
Had she a brother?
Or was there a dearer one
Still, and a nearer one
Yet, than all other?

Alas! for the rarity
Of Christian charity
Under the sun!
Oh, it was pitiful!
Near a whole city full,
Home she had none.

Sisterly, brotherly,
Fatherly, motherly
Feelings had changed:
Love, by harsh evidence
Thrown from its eminence
Even God's providence
Seeming estranged.

Where the lamps quiver
So far in the river,
With many a light
From window and casement
From garret to basement
She stood, with amazement
Houseless by night.

The bleak wind of March
Made her tremble and shiver;
But not the dark arch,

Or the black flowing river:
Mad from life's history,
Glad to death's mystery,
Swift to be hurled—
Anywhere, anywhere
Out of the world.

In she plunged boldly,
No matter how coldly
The rough river ran:
Over the brink of it,
Picture it—think of it,
Dissolute man!
Lave in it, drink of it
Then, if you can!

Take her up tenderly,
Lift her with care;
Fashioned so slenderly,
Young, and so fair!

Ere her limbs frigidly
Stiffen too rigidly,
Decently, kindly,
Smooth, and compose them;
And her eyes, close them,
Staring so blindly!

Dreadfully staring
Through muddy impurity,
And when with the daring
Last look of despairing
Fixed on futurity.

Perishing gloomily,
Spurned by contumely,
Cold inhumanity,
Burning insanity,
Into her rest.
Cross her hands humbly,

As if praying dumbly,
Over her breast.

Owning her weakness,
Her evil behavior,
And leaving, with meekness
Her sins to her Saviour.

NINTH TALE OF THE DECAMERON

by Boccaccio

Filomena had ceased speaking, and the queen, seeing that nobody was left to speak except Dioneo (who had his privilege) and herself, began cheerfully as follows:

You must know then that Coppo di Borghese Domenichi, who was and perhaps still is one of our fellow citizens, a man of great and revered authority in our days both from his manners and his virtues (far more than from nobility of blood), a most excellent person worthy of eternal fame, and in the fullness of his years delighted often to speak of past matters with his neighbours and other men. And this he could do better and more orderly and with a better memory and more ornate speech than anyone else.

Among other excellent things, he was wont to say that in the past there was in Florence a young man named Federigo, the son of Messer Filippo Alberighi, renowned above all other young gentlemen of Tuscany for his prowess in arms and his courtesy. Now, as most often happens to gentlemen, he fell in love with a lady named Monna Giovanna, in her time held to be one of the gayest and most beautiful women ever known in Florence. To win her love, he went to jousts and tourneys, made and gave feasts, and spent his money without stint. But she, no less chaste than beautiful, cared nothing for the things he did for her nor for him who did them.

Now as Federigo was spending far beyond his means and getting nothing in, as easily happens, his wealth failed and he remained poor with nothing but a little farm, on whose produce he lived very penuriously, and one falcon which was among the best in the world. More in love than ever, but thinking he would never be able to live in the town any more as he desired, he went to Campi where his farm was. There he spent his time hawking, asked nothing of nobody, and patiently endured his poverty.

Now while Federigo was in this extremity it happened one day that Monna Giovanna's husband fell ill, and seeing death come upon him, made his will. He was a very rich man and left his estate to a son who was already growing up. And then, since he had greatly loved Monna Giovanna, he made her his heir in case his son should die without legitimate children; and so he died.

Monna Giovanna was now a widow, and as is customary with our women, she went with her son to spend the year in a country house she had near Federigo's farm. The boy happened to strike up a friendship with Federigo, and delighted in dogs and hawks. He often saw Federigo's falcon fly, and took such great delight in it that he very much wanted to have it, but did not dare ask for it, since he saw how much Federigo prized it.

While matters were in this state, the boy fell ill. His mother was very much grieved, as he was her only child and she loved him extremely. She spent the day beside him, trying to help him, and often asked him if there was anything he wanted, begging him to say so, for if it were possible to have it, she would try to get it for him. After she had many times made this offer, the boy said, "Mother, if you can get me Federigo's falcon, I think I should soon be better."

The lady paused a little at this, and began to think what she should do. She knew that Federigo had loved her for a long time, and yet had never had one glance from her, and she said to herself, "How can I send or go and ask for this falcon, which is, from what I hear, the best that ever flew, and moreover his support in life? How can I be so thoughtless as to take this away from a gentleman who has no other pleasure in life?"

Although she was certain to have the bird for the asking, she remained in embarrassed thought, not knowing what to say, and did not answer her son. But at length love for her child got the upper hand and she determined that to please him in whatever way it might be, she would not send, but go herself for it and bring it back to him. So she replied, "Be comforted, my child, and try to get better somehow. I promise you that tomorrow morning I will go for it, and bring it to you."

The child was so delighted that he became a little better that same day. And on the morrow the lady took another woman to accompany her, and as if walking for exercise went to Federigo's cottage, and asked for him. Since it was not the weather for it, he had not been hawking for some days, and was in his garden. When he heard that Monna Giovanna was asking for him at the door, he was greatly astonished, and ran there happily. When she saw him coming, she got up to greet him with womanly charm, and when Federigo had courteously saluted her, she said. "How do you do, Federigo? I have come here to make amends for the damage you have suffered through me by loving me more than was needed. And in token of this, I intend to dine today familiarly with you and my companion here."

"Madonna," replied Federigo humbly, "I do not remember ever to have suffered any damage through you, but received so much good that if I was ever worth anything it was owing to your worth and the love I bore it. Your generous visit to me is so precious to me that I could spend again all that I have spent; but you have come to a poor host."

So saying, he modestly took her into his house, and from there to his garden. Since there was nobody else to remain in her company, he said, "Madonna, since there is nobody else, this good woman, the wife of this workman, will keep you company, while I go to set the table."

Now, although his poverty was extreme, he had never before realised what necessity he had fallen into by his foolish extravagance in spending his wealth. But he repented of it that morning when he could find nothing with which to do the honour to the lady, for love of whom he had entertained vast numbers of men in the past. In his anguish he cursed himself and his fortune and ran up and down like a man out of his senses, unable to find money or anything to pawn. The hour was late and his desire to honour the lady extreme, yet he would not apply to anyone else, even to his own workman; when suddenly his eye fell upon his falcon, perched on a bar in his sitting room. Having no one to whom he could appeal, he took the bird, and finding it plump, decided it would be food worthy such a lady. So, without further thought, he wrung its neck, made his little maid servant quickly pluck and prepare it, and put it on a spit to roast. He spread the table with the whitest napery, of which he had some left, and he returned to the lady in the garden with a cheerful face, saying that the meal he had been able to prepare for her was ready.

The lady and her companion arose and went to table, and there together with Federigo, who served it with the greatest devotion, they ate the good falcon. They left the table and spent some time in cheerful conversation, and the lady, thinking the time had now come to say what she had come for, spoke fairly to Federigo as follows: "Federigo, when you remember your former life and my chastity, which no doubt you considered harshness and cruelty, I have no doubt that you will be surprised at my presumption when you hear what I have come here for. But if you had children, I am sure that you would to some extent excuse me. I have come to ask you—against my will, and against all good manners and duty—for a gift, of which I know is something especially dear to you, and reasonably so, because I know your straitened fortune has left you no other pleasure. This gift is your falcon, which has so fascinated my child that if I do not take it to him, I am afraid his present illness will grow so much worse that I may lose him. Therefore I beg you, not by the love you bear me, but by your own nobleness, which has shown itself so much greater in all courteous usage than is wont in other men, that you will be pleased to give it to me, so that through this gift I may be able to say that I have saved my child's life, and thus be ever under an obligation to you."

When Federigo heard the lady's request, he began to weep in her presence, for he could not speak a word. The lady at first thought that his grief came from having to part with his good falcon, rather than from anything else, and she was almost on the point of retraction. But she remained firm and waited for Federigo's reply after his lamentation. And he said, "Madonna, ever since it has pleased God that I should set my love upon you, I have felt that Fortune has been contrary to me in many things, and have grieved for it. But they are all light in comparison with what She has done to me now, and I shall be never be at peace with Her again when I reflect that you came to my poor house, which you never deigned to visit when it was rich, and asked me for a little gift, and Fortune has so acted that I cannot give it to you. Why this cannot be, I will briefly tell you. When I heard that you in your graciousness desired to dine with me and I thought of your excellence and your worthiness, I thought it right and fitting to honour you with the best food I could obtain; so, remembering the falcon you ask me for and its value, I thought it a meal worthy of you, and today you had it roasted on the dish and set forth as best I could. But now I see you wanted the bird in another form, it is such a grief to me that I cannot serve you that I think I shall never be at peace again."

And after saying this, he showed her the feathers and the feet and the beak of the bird in proof. When the lady heard and saw all this, she first blamed him for having killed such a falcon to make a meal for a woman; and then she inwardly commended his greatness of soul which no poverty could or would be able to abate. But, having lost all hope in obtaining the falcon, and thus perhaps the health of her son, she departed sadly and returned to the child. Now, either from disappointment at not having the falcon or because his sickness must inevitably have led to it, the child died not many days later, to the mother's extreme grief.

She spent some time in tears and bitterness, yet, since she had been left very rich and was still young, her brothers often urged her to marry again. She did not want to do so, but as they kept pressing her, she remembered the worthiness of Federigo and his last act of generosity, in killing such a falcon to do her honour.

"I will gladly submit to marriage when you please," she said to her brothers, "but if you want me to take a husband, I will take no man but Federigo degli Alberighi."

At this her brothers laughed at her, saying, "Why, what are you talking about, you fool? Why do you want a man who hasn't a penny in the world?"

"Brothers, I know it is as you say," she replied, "But I would rather have a man who needs money than money which needs a man."

Seeing her determination, the brothers, who knew Federigo's good qualities, did as she wanted, and gave her with all her wealth to him, in spite of his poverty. Federigo, finding that he had such a woman, whom he loved so much, with all her wealth to boot, as his wife, was more prudent with his money in the future, and ended his days happily with her.

SUMMARY:

1. A young man named Federigo fell in love with a beautiful woman named Monna, and spent his modest fortune wooing her, to no avail. She married another man.

2. Federigo was living the modest life of a farmer when Monna's husband fell ill. A very rich man, he left his fortune to his young son; in the event of the son's death, Monna would get the fortune.

3. Monna and her son spent a year at their country house near Federigo's farm, and the boy became friends with the farmer, who had a very special falcon that both boy and man prized.

4. Eventually, the boy fell ill. His mother asked him what would make him better, and he replied that Federigo's falcon might help him get well.

5. Monna knew Federigo loved her, and would do anything for her, but she was loathe to take his most loved possession. Still, she loved her son, so she went.

6. Federigo, surprised and overjoyed at the visit, could find nothing to serve the fine lady. Finally, he spied the falcon; he bade his maid pluck and prepare it, and served it for lunch.

7. At the table, the lady made her request, and Federigo began to weep. He told her the falcon had been given her in another form. At first the lady was angry with him, then realized how noble he had been to try to honor her with such a meal.

8. Whether from sickness or disappointment, the child died, much to the mother's grief. But soon, her brothers urged her to marry again, since she

was still young and rich. As her new husband, she chose Federigo.

ENEMIES

by Tim O'Brien

One morning in late July, while we were out on patrol near LZ Gator, Lee Strunk and Dave Jensen got into a fistfight. It was about something stupid—a missing jackknife—but even so the fight was vicious. For a while it went back and forth, but Dave Jensen was much bigger and much stronger, and eventually he wrapped an arm around Strunk's neck and pinned him down and kept hitting him on the nose. Strunk's nose made a sharp snapping sound, like a firecracker, but even then Jensen kept hitting him, over and over. It took three of us to pull him off. When it was over, Strunk had to be choppered back to the rear. Two days later he rejoined us wearing a metal splint and lots of gauze. In any other circumstance it might've ended there. But this was Vietnam, where guys carried guns, and Dave Jensen started to worry. There were no threats, no vows of revenge, just a silent tension between them that made Jenson take special precautions. On patrol he was careful to keep track of Strunk's whereabouts. He dug his foxhole on the far side of the perimeter; he kept his back covered; he avoided situations that might put the two of them alone together. After a week of this, the strain began to create problems. Jenson couldn't relax. Like fighting two different wars, he said. No safe ground: enemies everywhere. No front or rear. At night he had trouble sleeping—a skittish feeling—always on guard, hearing strange noises in the dark, imagining a grenade rolling into his foxhole or the tickle of a knife against his ear. The distinction between good guys and bad guys disappeared for him. Even in times of relative safety, while the rest of us took it easy, Jensen would sit with his back against a tree, weapon across his knees, watching Lee Strunk with quick, nervous eyes. One afternoon he finally snapped and began firing his weapon in the air, yelling Strunk's name, just firing and yelling, and it didn't stop until he'd rattled off an entire magazine of ammunition. We were all flat on the ground. Nobody had the nerve to go near him. Jensen started to reload, but then suddenly he sat down and held his head in his arms and wouldn't move. For two or three hours he simply sat there.

But that wasn't the bizarre part.

Because late that same night he borrowed a pistol, gripped it by the barrel, and used it like a hammer to break his own nose.

Afterward, he crossed the perimeter to Lee Strunk's foxhole. He showed him what he'd done and asked if everything was square between them.

Strunk nodded and said, Sure, things were square.

But in the morning Lee Strunk couldn't stop laughing. "The man's crazy," he said. "I stole his fucking jackknife."

A ROSE FOR EMILY

by William Faulkner

When Miss Emily Grierson died, our whole town went to her funeral; the men through a sort of respectful affection for a fallen monument, the women mostly out of curiosity to see the inside of her house, which no one save an old manservant—a combined gardener and cook—had seen in at least ten years.

It was a big squarish frame house that had once been white, decorated with cupolas and spires and scrolled balconies in the heavily lightsome style of the seventies, set on what had once been our most select street. But garages and cotton gins had encroached and obliterated the august names of that neighborhood, and only Miss Emily's house was left, lifting its stubborn and coquettish decay above the cotton wagons and the gasoline pumps—an eyesore among eyesores.

Alive, Miss Emily had been a sort of hereditary obligation upon the town, dating from that day in 1894 when Colonel Sartoris, the mayor—he who fathered the edict that no Negro woman should appear on the street without an apron—remitted her taxes, the dispensation dating from the death of her father on into perpetuity. Not that Miss Emily would have accepted charity. Colonel Sartoris invented an involved tale to the effect that Miss Emily's father had loaned money to the town, which the town, as a matter of business, preferred this way of repaying. Only a man of Colonel Sartoris' generation and thought could have invented it, and only a woman could have believed it.

When the next generation, with its more modern ideas, became mayors and aldermen, this arrangement created some little dissatisfaction. A deputation waited on her, knocked at the door through which no visitor had passed since she ceased giving china-painting lessons eight or ten years earlier. They were admitted by the old Negro into a dim hall from which a stairway mounted into still more shadow. It smelled of dust and disuse—a close, dank smell. The Negro led them into a parlor. It was furnished in heavy, leather-covered furniture. When the Negro opened the blinds of one window, they could see that the leather was cracked; and when they sat down, a faint dust rose sluggishly about their thighs, spinning with slow motes in the single sun-ray. On a tarnished gilt easel before the fireplace stood a crayon portrait of Miss Emily's father.

They rose when she entered—a small, fat woman in black, with a thin, gold chain descending to her waist and vanishing into her belt, leaning on an ebony cane with a tarnished gold head. She looked bloated, like a body long submerged in motionless water, and of that pallid hue. Her eyes, lost in the fatty ridges of her face, looked like two small pieces of coal pressed into a lump of dough as they moved from one face to another while the visitors stated their errand.

She did not ask them to sit. She just stood in the door and listened quietly until the spokesman came to a stumbling halt. Then they could hear the invisible watch ticking at the end of the gold chain.

Her voice was dry and cold. "I have no taxes in Jefferson. Colonel Sartoris explained it to me. Perhaps one of you can gain access to the city records and satisfy yourselves."

"But we have. We are the city authorities, Miss Emily. Didn't you get a notice from the sheriff, signed by him?"

"I received a paper, yes," Miss Emily said. "Perhaps he considers himself the sheriff. . .I have no taxes in Jefferson."

"But there is nothing on the books to show that, you see. We must go by the—"

"See Colonel Sartoris. I have no taxes in Jefferson."

"But Miss Emily—"

"See Colonel Sartoris." (Colonel Sartoris had been dead almost ten years.) "I have no taxes in Jefferson. Tobe!" The Negro appeared. "Show these gentlemen out."

So she vanquished them, just as she had vanquished their fathers thirty years before about the smell. That was two years after her father's death and a short time after her sweetheart—the one we believed would marry her—had deserted her. After her father's death she went out very little; after her sweetheart went away, people hardly saw her at all. A few of the ladies had the temerity to call, but were not received, and the only sign of life about the place was the Negro man—a young man then—going in and out with a market basket.

"Just as if a man—any man—could keep a kitchen properly," the ladies said; so they were not surprised when the smell developed. It was another link between the gross, teeming world and the high and mighty Griersons.

A neighbor, a woman, complained to the mayor, Judge Stevens, eighty years old.

"But what will you have me do about it, madam?" he said.

"Why, send her word to stop it," the woman said. "Isn't there a law?"

"I'm sure that won't be necessary," Judge Stevens said. "It's probably just a snake or rat that nigger of hers killed in the yard. I'll speak to him about it."

The next day he received two more complaints, one from a man who came in diffident deprecation. "We really must do something about it, Judge. I'd be the last one in the world to bother Miss Emily, but we've got to do something." That night the Board of Aldermen went met—three graybeards and one younger man, a member of the riding generation.

"It's simple enough," he said. "Send her word to have her place cleaned up. Give her a certain time to do it in, and if she don't . . ."

"Dammit, sir," Judge Stevens said. "Will you accuse a lady to her face of smelling bad?"

So the next night, after midnight, four men crossed Miss Emily's lawn and slunk about the house like burglars, sniffing along the base of the brickwork and at the cellar openings while one of them performed a regular sowing motion with his hand out of a sack slung from his shoulder. They broke open the cellar door and sprinkled lime there, and in all the outbuildings. As they recrossed the lawn, a window that had been dark was lighted and Miss Emily sat in it, the light behind her, and her upright torso motionless as that of an idol. They crept quietly across the lawn and into the shadow of the locusts that lined the street. After a week or two, the smell went away.

That was when people had begun to feel really sorry for her. People in our town, remembering how old lady Wyatt, her great-aunt, had gone completely crazy at last, believed that the Griersons held themselves a little too high for what they really were. None of the young men were quite good enough for Miss Emily and such. We had long thought of them as a tableau, Miss Emily a slender figure in white in the background, her father a spraddled silhouette in the foreground, his back to her and clutching a horsewhip, the two of them framed by the back-flung front door. So when she got to be thirty and still single, we were not pleased exactly, but vindicated; even with insanity in the family she wouldn't have turned down all her chances if they had really materialized.

When her father died, it got about that the house was all that was left to her; and in a way, people were glad. At last they could pity Miss Emily. Being left alone, and a pauper, she had become humanized. Now she too would know the old thrill and the old despair of a penny more or less.

The day after his death all the ladies prepared to call at the house and offer condolence and aid, as is our custom. Miss Emily met them at the door, dressed as usual and with no trace of grief on her face. She told them that her father was not dead. She did that for three days, with the ministers calling on her, and the doctors, trying to persuade her to let them dispose of the body. Just as they were about to resort to law and force, she broke down, and they buried her father quickly.

We did not say she was crazy then. We believed she had to do that. We remembered all the young men her father had driven away, and we knew that with nothing left, she would have to cling to that which had robbed her, as people will.

She was sick for a long time. When we saw her again, her hair was cut short, making her look like a girl, with a vague resemblance to those angels in colored church windows—sort of tragic and serene.

The town had just let the contracts for paving the sidewalks, and in the summer after her father's death they began to work. The construction company came with the niggers and mules and machinery, and a foreman named Homer Barron, a Yankee—a big, dark, ready man, with a big voice and eyes lighter than his face. The little boys would follow in groups to hear him cuss the niggers, and the niggers singing in time to the rise and fall of the picks. Pretty soon he knew everybody in town. Whenever you heard a lot of laughing anywhere about the square, Homer Barron would be in the center of the group. Presently we began to see him and Miss Emily on Sunday afternoons driving in the yellow-wheeled buggy and the matched team of bays from the livery stable.

At first we were glad that Miss Emily would have an interest, because the ladies all said, "Of course a Grierson would not think seriously of a Northerner, a day laborer." But there were still others, older people, who said that even grief could not cause a real lady to forget noblesse oblige—without calling it noblesse oblige. They just said, "Poor Emily. Her kinsfolk should come to her." She had some kin in Alabama; but years ago her father had fallen out with them over the estate of old lady Wyatt, the crazy woman, and there was no communication between the two families. They had not even been represented at the funeral.

And as soon as the old people said, "Poor Emily," the whispering began. "Do you suppose it's really so?" they said to one another. "Of course it is. What else could . . ." This behind their hands; rustling of silk and satin behind jalousies closed upon the sun of Sunday afternoon as the thin, swift clop-clop-clop of the matched team passed: "Poor Emily."

She carried her head high enough—even when we believed that she was fallen. It was as if she demanded more than ever the recognition of her dignity as the last Grierson; as if it had wanted that touch of earthiness to reaffirm her imperviousness. Like when she bought that rat poison, the arsenic. That was over a year after they had begun to say, "Poor Emily," and while the two female cousins were visiting her.

"I want some poison," she said to the druggist. She was over thirty then, still a slight woman, though thinner than usual, with cold, haughty black eyes.

"Yes, Miss Emily. What kind? For rats and such? I'd recom—"

"I want the best you have. I don't care what kind."

The druggist named several. "They'll kill anything up to an elephant. But what you want is—"

"Arsenic," Miss Emily said. "Is that a good one?"

"Yes, ma'am. But what you want—"

"I want arsenic."

The druggist looked down at her. She looked back at him, erect, her face like a strained flag. "Why, of course," the druggist said. "If that's what you want. But the law requires you to tell me what you are going to use it for."

Miss Emily just stared at him, her head tilted back in order to look him eye for eye, until he looked away and went and got the arsenic and wrapped it up. The Negro delivery boy brought her the package; the druggist didn't come back. When she opened the package at home there was written on the box, under the skull and bones: "For rats."

So the next day we all said, "She will kill herself;" and we said it would be the best thing. When she was first seen with Homer Barron, we had said, "She will marry him." Then we said, "She will persuade him yet," because Homer himself had remarked—he liked men, and it was known that he drank with the younger men in the Elks' Club—that he was not a marrying man. Later we said, "Poor Emily" behind the jalousies as they passed on Sunday afternoon in the glittering buggy, Miss Emily with her head high and Homer Barron with his hat cocked and a cigar in his teeth, reins and whip in a yellow glove.

Then some of the ladies began to say that it was a disgrace to the town and a bad example to the young people. The men did not want to interfere, but at last the ladies forced the Baptist minister—Miss Emily's people were Episcopal—to call upon her. He would never divulge what happened during that interview, but he refused to go back again. The next Sunday they again drove about the streets, and the following day the minister's wife wrote to Miss Emily's relations in Alabama.

So she had blood-kin under her roof again and we sat back to watch the developments. At first nothing happened. Then we were sure that they were to be married. We learned that Miss Emily had been to the jeweler's and ordered a man's toilet in silver, with the letters H. B. on each piece. Two days later we learned that she had bought a complete outfit of men's clothing, including a nightshirt, and we said, "They are married." We were really glad. We were glad because the two female cousins were even more Grierson than Miss Emily had ever been.

So we were not surprised when Homer Barron—the streets had finished some time since—was gone. We were a little disappointed that there was not a public blowing-off, but we believed that he had gone on to prepare for Miss Emily's coming, or to give her a chance to get rid of the cousins. (By that time it was a cabal, and we were all Miss Emily's allies to help circumvent the cousins.) Sure enough, after another week they departed. And, as we had expected all along, within three days

Homer Barron was back in town. A neighbor saw the Negro man admit him at the kitchen door at dusk one evening.

And that was the last we saw of Homer Barron. And of Miss Emily for some time. The Negro man went in and out with the market basket, but the front door remained closed. Now and then we would see her at a window for a moment, as the men did that night when they sprinkled the lime, but for almost six months she did not appear on the streets. Then we knew that this was to be expected too; as if that quality of her father which had thwarted her woman's life so many times had been too virulent and too furious to die.

When we next saw Miss Emily, she had grown fat and her hair was turning gray. During the next few years it grew grayer and grayer until it attained an even pepper-and-salt iron-gray, when it ceased turning. Up to the day of her death at seventy-four it was still that iron-gray, like the hair of an active man.

From that time on her front door remained closed, save for a period of six or seven years, when she was about forty, during which she gave lessons in china-painting. She fitted up a studio in one of the downstairs room, where the daughters and granddaughters of Colonel Sartoris' contemporaries were sent to her with the same regularity and in the same spirit that they were sent to church on Sundays with a twenty-five-cent piece for the collection plate. Meanwhile her taxes had been remitted.

Then the newer generation became the backbone and the spirit of the town, and the painting pupils grew up and fell away and did not send their children to her with boxes of color and brushes and pictures cut from the ladies' magazines. The front door closed upon the last one and remained closed for good. When the town got free postal delivery, Miss Emily alone refused to let them fasten the metal numbers above her door and attach a mailbox to it. She would not listen to them.

Daily, monthly, yearly, we watched the Negro grow grayer and more stooped, going in and out with the market basket. Each December we sent her a tax notice, which would be returned by the post office one week later, unclaimed. Now and then we would see her in one of the downstairs windows—she had evidently shut up the top floor of the house—like the torso of an idol in a niche, looking or not looking at us, we could never tell which. Thus she passed from generation to genera-tion—dear, inescapable, tranquil, and perverse.

And so she died. Fell ill in the house filled with dust and shadows, with only a doddering Negro man to wait on her. We did not even know she was sick; we had long since given up trying to get any infor-mation from the Negro. He had talked to no one, probably not even to her, for his voice had grown harsh and rusty, as if from disuse.

She died in one of the downstairs rooms, in a heavy walnut bed with a curtain, her gray hair propped on a pillow yellow and moldy with age and lack of sunlight.

The Negro met the first of the ladies at the front door and let them in, with their hushed, hissing voices and their quick, curious glances, and then he disappeared. He walked right through the house and out the back and was never seen again.

The two female cousins came back at once. They held the funeral on the second day, with the town coming to look at Miss Emily beneath a mass of bought flowers, with the face of her father musing profoundly above the bier and the ladies sibilant and macabre; and the very old men—some in their brushed Confederate uniforms—on the porch and the lawn, talking of Miss Emily as if she had been a contemporary of theirs, believing they had danced with her and courted her perhaps, confusing time with its mathematical progression, as the old do.

Already we knew that there was one room in that region above stairs which no one had seen in forty years, and which would have to be forced open. We waited until Miss Emily was decently in the ground before opening the door.

The violence of breaking down the door seemed to fill this room with pervading dust. A thin, acrid pall as of the tomb lay everywhere upon this room decked and furnished as for a bridal: upon the valance curtains of faded rose color, upon the rose-shaded lights, upon the dressing table, upon the delicate array of crystal and the man's toilet things backed with silver so tarnished that the monogram was obscured. Among them lay a collar and tie, as if they had just been removed, which, lifted, left upon the surface a pale crescent in the dust. Upon a chair hung the suit, carefully folded; beneath it two mute shoes and the discarded socks.

The man himself lay in the bed.

For a long while we just stood there, looking down at the profound and fleshless grin. The body had apparently once lain in the attitude of an embrace, but now the long sleep that outlasts love, that conquers even the grimace of love, had cuckolded him. What was left of him, rotted beneath what was left of the nightshirt, had become inextricable from the bed in which he lay; and upon him and upon the pillow beside him lay that even coating of the patient and biding dust.

Then we noticed that in the second pillow was the indentation of a head. One of us lifted something from it, and leaning forward, that faint and invisible dust dry and acrid in the nostrils, we saw a long strand of iron-gray hair.

SUMMARY:

1. Miss Emily was always an enigma in the town. In the years before her death, no one had seen her— only her manservant coming and going from her house.

2. Just before she died, the town fathers visited her to collect taxes, and found a small, fat woman dressed in black, who stubbornly refused to pay, citing an old dispensation that had been granted to her shortly after her father had died. The dispensation, granted out of charity, nulled her taxes. She banished the collectors, just as she had banished their fathers years before when they came to her about the smell.

3. The smell was first noticed several days after her suitor disappeared, and could not be dissipated. Several men snuck up to the house to find its source, but could locate nothing. Eventually, the smell disappeared.

4. Miss Emily had once been slender and young, and had been wooed but never married. At her

father's death, she refused to have him buried; it was only when the doctors and ministers threatened force that she relented. It was then we all began to suspect she was crazy.

5. She was sick for a long time after that, then the dapper foreman Homer Barron began to court her. The two could be seen riding about town in Barron's buggy, and we all suspected they would soon marry.

6. One day, Emily was seen purchasing rat poison - arsenic. Soon after, Homer Barron was heard at the local Elks Club proclaiming he was not a marrying man. When Emily purchased a man's silver grooming set and nightshirt, we assumed they were married. Then, Homer Barron disappeared.

7. We did not see her again for many years, not even when the men went to her house to find the source of the smell. When we did see her, her hair had gone grey and she had grown fat. For a short time, she gave china painting lessons. But when the mothers stopped sending their girls, Miss Emily faded out of sight.

8. Eventually, she fell ill and died. She died in a downstairs bedroom, which is where we found her. Some of the ladies of the town, along with her cousins, began to settle her affairs.

9. There was a room upstairs in the house that had been unexplored for forty years, and we had to force the door. Inside, we found a bedroom decorated as a bridal chamber. A man's silver grooming set lay on the dresser, a man's clothing folded carefully over the chair.

10. In the bed lay the man himself. Apparently, he had once lain in an embrace. On the pillow next to his, there was the indentation of a head, and a long strand of iron-gray hair.

FROM MY ÁNTONIA

by Willa Cather

When Pavel and Peter were young men, living at home in Russia, they were asked to be groomsmen for a friend who was to marry the belle of another village. It was in the dead of winter and the groom's party went over to the wedding in sledges. Peter and Pavel drove in the groom's sledge, and six sledges followed with all his relatives and friends.

After the ceremony at the church, the party went to a dinner given by the parents of the bride. The dinner lasted all afternoon; then it became a supper and continued far into the night. There was much dancing and drinking. At midnight the parents of the bride said good-bye to her and blessed her. The groom took her up in his arms and carried her out to his sledge and tucked her under the blankets. He sprang in beside her, and Pavel and Peter (our Pavel and Peter!) took the front seat. Pavel drove. The party set out with singing and the jingle of sleigh-bells, the groom's sledge going first. All the drivers were more or less the worse for merry-making, and the groom was absorbed in his bride.

The wolves were bad that winter, and everyone knew it, yet when they heard the first wolf-cry, the drivers were not much alarmed. They had too much good food and drink inside them. The first howls were taken up and echoed and with quickening repetitions. The wolves were coming together. There was no moon, but the starlight was clear on the snow. A black drove came up over the hill behind the wedding party. The wolves ran like streaks of shadow; they looked no bigger than dogs, but there were hundreds of them.

Something happened to the hindmost sledge: the driver lost control—he was probably very drunk—the horses left the road, the sledge was caught in a clump of trees, and overturned. The occupants rolled out over the snow, and the fleetest of the wolves sprang upon them. The shrieks that followed made everybody sober. The drivers stood up and lashed their horses. The groom had the best team and his sledge was lightest—all the others carried from six to a dozen people.

Another driver lost control. The screams of the horses were more terrible to hear than the cries of the men and women. Nothing seemed to check the wolves. It was hard to tell what was happening in the rear; the people who were falling behind shrieked as piteously as those who were already lost. The little bride hid her face on the groom's shoulder and sobbed. Pavel sat still and watched his horses. The road was clear and white, and the groom's three blacks went like the wind. It was only necessary to be calm and to guide them carefully.

At length, as they breasted a long hill, Peter rose cautiously and looked back. "There are only three sledges left," he whispered.

"And the wolves?" Pavel asked.

"Enough! Enough for all of us."

Pavel reached the brow of the hill, but only two sledges followed him down the other side. In that moment on the hilltop, they saw behind them a whirling black group on the snow. Presently the groom screamed. He saw his father's sledge overturned, with his mother and sisters. He sprang up as if he meant to jump, but the girl shrieked and held him back. It was even then too late. The black ground-shadows were already crowding over the heap in the road, and one horse ran out across the fields, his harness hanging to him, wolves at his heels. But the groom's movement had given Pavel an idea.

They were within a few miles of their village now. The only sledge left out of six was not very far behind them, and Pavel's middle horse was failing. Beside a frozen pond something happened to the other sledge; Peter saw it plainly. Three big wolves got abreast of the horses, and the horses went crazy. They tried to jump over each other, got tangled up in the harness, and overturned the sledge.

When the shrieking behind them died away, Pavel realized that he was alone upon the familiar road. ``They still come?" he asked Peter.

"Yes."

"How may?"

"Twenty, thirty—enough."

Now his middle horse was being almost dragged by the other two. Pavel gave Peter the reins and stepped carefully into the back of the sledge. He called to the groom that they must lighten—and pointed to the bride. The young man cursed him and held her tighter. Pavel tried to drag her away. In the struggle, the groom rose. Pavel knocked him over the side of the sledge and threw the girl after him. He said he never remembered exactly how he did it, or what happened afterward. Peter, crouching in the front seat, saw nothing. The first thing either of them noticed was a new sound that broke into the clear air, louder than they had ever heard it before—the bell of the monastery of their own village, ringing for early prayers.

Pavel and Peter drove into the village alone, and they had been alone ever since. They were run out of their village. Pavel's own mother would not look at him. They went away to strange towns, but when people learned where they came from, they were always asked if they were the two men who had fed the bride to the wolves. Wherever they went, the story followed them. It took them five years to save money enough to come to America. They worked in Chicago, Des Moines, Fort Wayne, but they were always unfortunate. When Pavel's health grew so bad, they decided to try farming.

Pavel died a few days after he unburdened his mind to a friend, and was buried in the Norwegian graveyard. Peter sold off everything, and left the country—went to be cook in a railway construction camp where gangs of Russians were employed.

OCCURRENCE AT OWL CREEK BRIDGE

by Ambrose Bierce

A man stood upon a railroad bridge in northern Alabama, looking down into the swift water twenty feet below. The man's hands were behind his back, the wrists bound with a cord. A rope encircled his neck. It was attached to a stout cross-timber above his head and the slack fell to the level of his knees. Some loose boards laid upon the sleepers supporting the metals of the railway supplied a footing for him and his executioners—two private soldiers of the Federal army, directed by a sergeant who in civil life may have been a deputy sheriff. Close upon the temporary platform was an officer in the uniform of his rank, armed. He was a captain. A sentinel at each end of the bridge stood with his rifle held vertical in front of the left shoulder, the hammer resting on the forearm thrown straight across the chest—a formal and unnatural position, enforcing an erect carriage of the body. It did not appear to be the duty of these two men to know what was occurring at the centre of the bridge; they merely blockaded the two ends of the foot planking that traversed it.

Beyond one of the sentinels nobody was in sight. The railroad ran straight away into a forest for a hundred yards, then, curving, was lost to view. Doubtless there was an outpost farther along. The other bank of the stream was open ground—a gentle acclivity topped with a stockade of vertical tree trunks, loopholed for rifles, with a single embrasure through which protruded the muzzles of brass cannon commanding the bridge. Midway up the slope between the bridge and fort were the spectators—a single company of infantry in line, at "parade rest," the butts of the rifles on the ground, the barrels inclining slightly backward against the right shoulder, the hands crossed upon the stock. A lieutenant stood at the right of the line, the point of his sword upon the ground, his left hand resting upon his right. Excepting the group of four at the centre of the bridge, not a man moved. The company faced the bridge, staring stonily, motionless. The sentinels, facing the banks of the stream, might have been statues to adorn the bridge. The captain stood with folded arms, silent, observing the work of his subordinates, but making no sign. Death is a dignitary who when he comes announced is to be received with formal regard, even by those most familiar with him. In the code of military etiquette silence and fixity are forms of deference.

The man being hanged was thirty-five years of age. He was a civilian planter. His features were good—a straight nose, firm mouth, broad forehead, from which his long, dark hair was combed straight back, falling behind his ears to the collar of his well-fitting frock-coat. He wore a mustache and pointed beard, but no whiskers; his eyes were large and dark gray, and had a kindly expression which one would hardly have expected in one whose neck was in the hemp. Evidently this was no vulgar assassin. The liberal military code makes for provisions for hanging many persons.

The preparations complete, the two private soldiers stepped aside and each drew away the plank upon which he had been standing. The sergeant turned to the captain, saluted and placed himself immediately behind that officer, who in turn moved apart one pace. These movements left the condemned man and the sergeant standing on the two ends of the same plank, which spanned three of the cross-ties of the bridge. The end upon which the civilian stood almost, but not quite, reached a fourth. This plank had been held in place by the weight of the captain; it was now held by that of the sergeant. At a signal from the former the latter would step aside, the plank would tilt and the condemned man go down between the two ties. The arrangement commended itself to his judgment as simple and effective. His face had not been covered nor his eyes bandaged. He looked a moment at his footing, then let his gaze wander to the swirling water of the stream racing madly beneath his feet. A piece of dancing driftwood caught his attention and his eyes followed it down the current. How slowly it appeared to move! What a sluggish stream!

He closed his eyes in order to fix his last thoughts upon his wife and children. The water, touched to gold by the early sun, the brooding mists under the banks at some distance down the stream, the fort, the soldiers, the piece of drift—all had distracted him. And now he became conscious of a new disturbance. Striking through the thought of his dear ones was a sound which he could neither ignore or understand, a sharp, distinct, metallic percussion like a stroke of a blacksmith's hammer upon the anvil; it had the same ringing quality. He wondered what it was, and whether immeasurably distant or near by—it seemed both. Its recurrence was regular, but as slow as the tolling of a death knell. He awaited each stroke with impatience and—he knew not why—apprehension. The intervals of silence grew progressively longer; the delays became maddening. With their greater infrequency the sounds increased in strength and sharpness. They hurt his ear like the thrust of a knife; he feared he would shriek. What he heard was the ticking of his own watch.

He unclosed his eyes and saw the water below him. "If I could free my hands," he thought, "I might throw off the noose and spring into the stream. By diving I could evade the bullets and, swimming vigorously, reach the bank, take to the woods, and get away home. My home, thank God, is as yet outside their lines; my wife and little ones are still beyond the invader's farthest advance."

As these thoughts flashed through the doomed man's brain, the captain nodded to the sergeant. The sergeant stepped aside.

Peyton Farquhar was a well-to-do planter, of an old and highly respected Alabama family. Being a slave owner and like other slave owners a politician, he was naturally a secessionist and ardently devoted to the Southern cause. Circumstances of an imperious nature had prevented him from taking service with the gallant army that had fought the disastrous campaigns ending with the fall of Corinth, and he chafed under the inglorious restraint, longing for the release of his energies, the larger life of the soldier, the opportunity for distinction. That opportunity, he felt, would come, as it comes to all in war time. Meanwhile, he did what he could. No service was too humble for him to perform in the aid of the South, no adventure too perilous for him to undertake if it was consistent with the character of a civilian who was at heart a soldier, and who in good faith and without too much qualification assented to at least a part of the villainous dictum that all is fair in love and war.

One evening while Farquhar and his wife were sitting on a rustic bench near the entrance to his grounds, a gray-clad soldier rode up to the gate and asked for a drink of water. Mrs. Farquhar was only too happy to serve him with her own white hands. While she was fetching the water her husband approached the dusty horseman and inquired eagerly for news from the front.

"The Yanks are repairing the railroads," said the man, "and are getting ready for another advance. They have reached the Owl Creek bridge, put it in order and built a stockade on the north bank. The commandant has issued an order, which is posted everywhere, that any civilian caught interfering with the railroad, its bridges, tunnels or trains will be summarily hanged. I saw the order."

"How far is it to the Owl Creek bridge?" Farquhar asked.

"About thirty miles."

"Is there no force on this side of the creek?"

"Only a picket post half a mile out, on the railroad, and a single sentinel at this end of the bridge."

"Suppose a man—a civilian and student of hanging—should elude the picket post and perhaps get the better of the sentinel," said Farquhar, smiling, "What could he accomplish?"

The soldier reflected. "I was there a month ago," he replied. "I observed that the flood of last winter had lodged a great quantity of driftwood against the wooden pier at this end of the bridge. It is now dry and would burn like tow."

The lady had now brought the water, which the soldier drank. He thanked her ceremoniously, bowed to her husband and rode away. An hour later, after nightfall, he repassed the plantation, going northward in the direction from which he had come. He was a Federal scout.

As Peyton Farquhar plunged downward through the bridge he lost consciousness and was as one already dead. He was awakened—ages later, it seemed—by the pain of a sharp pressure upon his throat, followed by a sense of suffocation. Keen, poignant agonies, like streams of pulsating fire, shot from his neck downward through every fibre of his body. He was conscious of nothing but a feeling of fullness—of congestion. He was conscious only of motion, and seemed encompassed in a luminous cloud, of which he was now merely the fiery heart, without material substance. Then with terrible suddenness, the light about him shot upward with the noise of a loud splash; a frightful roaring was in his ears, and all was cold and dark. The power of thought was restored.

He knew that the rope had broken and he had fallen into the stream.

The noose about his neck was suffocating him and kept the water from his lungs. To die of hanging at the bottom of a river!—the idea seemed to him ludicrous. He opened his eyes in the darkness and saw above him a gleam of light, but how distant, how inaccessible! He was still sinking, for the light became fainter and fainter until it was a mere glimmer. Then it began to grow and brighten, and he knew that he was rising toward the surface—knew it with reluctance, for he was now very comfortable. "To be hanged and drowned," he thought, "That is not so bad; but I do not wish to be shot. No; I will not be shot; that is not fair."

He was not conscious of an effort, but a sharp pain in his wrist apprised him that he was trying to free his hands. He gave the struggle his attention, as an idler might observe the feat of a juggler, without interest in an outcome. What splendid effort! Ah, what a fine endeavor! Bravo! The cord fell away; his arms parted and floated upward, the hands dimly seen on each side in the growing light. He watched them with new interest as first one and then the other pounced upon the noose at his neck. They tore it away and thrust it fiercely aside, its undulations resembling those of a water snake. "Put it back, put it back!" He thought he shouted these words to his hands, for the undoing of the noose had been succeeded by the direst pang that he had yet experienced. His neck ached horribly; his brain was on fire; his heart, which had been fluttering faintly, gave a great leap, trying to force itself out at his mouth. His whole body was racked and wrenched with an unsupportable anguish! But his disobedient hands gave no heed to the command. They beat the water vigorously with quick, downward strokes, forcing him to the surface. He felt his head emerge; his eyes were blinded by the sunlight; his chest expanded convulsively, and with a supreme and crowning agony his lungs engulfed a great draught of air, which instantly he expelled in a shriek!

He was now in full possession of his physical senses. They were, indeed, preternaturally keen and alert. Something in the awful disturbance of his organic system had so exalted and refined them that they had made record of things never before perceived. He felt the ripples upon his face and heard their separate sounds as they struck. He looked at the forest on the bank of the steam, saw the individual trees, the leaves and the veining of each leaf—saw the very insects upon them: the locusts, the brilliant-bodied flies, the gray spiders stretching their webs from twig to twig. He noted the prismatic colors in all the dew-drops upon a million blades of grass. The humming of the gnats that danced above the eddies of the stream, the beating of the dragon-flies' wings, the strokes of the water spider's legs, like oars which had lifted their boat—all these made audible music. A fish slid along beneath his eyes and he heard the rush of its body parting the water.

He had come to the surface facing down the stream; in a moment the visible world seemed to wheel slowly round, himself the pivotal point, and he saw the bridge, the captain, the sergeant, the two privates, his executioners, silhouetted against the blue sky. They shouted and gesticulated, pointing at him. The captain had drawn his pistol, but did not fire; the others were unarmed. Their movements were grotesque and horrible, their forms gigantic.

Suddenly he heard a sharp report and something struck the water smartly within a few inches of his head, spattering his face with spray. He heard second report, and saw one of the sentinels with his rifle at his shoulder, blue smoke rising from the muzzle. The man in the water saw the eye of the man on the bridge gazing into his own through the sights of the rifle. He observed that it was a gray eye and remembered having read that gray eyes were keenest, and that all famous marksmen had them. Nevertheless, this one had missed.

A counter-swirl had caught Farquhar and turned him half around; he was again looking into the forest on the bank opposite the fort. The sound of a clear high voice in monotonous singsong now rang out behind him and came across the water with a distinctness that pierced and subdued all other sounds, even the beating of the ripples in the ears. Although no soldier, he had frequented camps enough to know the dread significance of that deliberate, drawling, aspirated chant; the lieutenant on shore was taking a part on the morning's work. How coldly and pitilessly—with what an even calm intonation, presaging, and enforcing tranquility in the men—with what accurately measured intervals fell those cruel words:

"Attention, company! . . . Shoulder arms! . . . Ready! . . . Aim! . . . Fire!"

Farquhar dived—dived as deeply as he could. The water roared in his ears like the voice of Niagara, yet he heard the dulled thunder of the volley and, rising again toward the surface, met shining bits of metal, singularly flattened, oscillating slowly downward. Some of them touched him on the face and hands, then fell away, continuing their descent. One lodged between his collar and neck: it was hot and he snatched it out.

As he rose to the surface, gasping for breath, he saw that he had been a long time under water; he was perceptibly farther down stream—nearer to safety. The soldiers had almost finished reloading; the metal ramrods flashed all at once in the sunshine as they were drawn from the barrels, turned in the air, and thrust into their sockets. The two sentinels fired again, independently and ineffectually.

The hunted man saw all this over his shoulder; he was now swimming vigorously with the current. His brain was as energetic as his arms and legs; he thought with the rapidity of lightning.

"The officer," he reasoned, "will not make that martinet's error a second time. It is as easy to dodge a volley as a single shot. He has already given the command to fire at will. God help me, I cannot dodge them all!"

An appalling splash within two yards of him was followed by a loud, rushing sound which seemed to travel back through the air to the fort and died in an explosion which stirred the very river to its deeps! A rising sheet of water curved over him, fell down upon him, blinded him, strangled him! The cannon had taken a hand in the game. As he shook his head free from the commotion of the smitten water he heard the deflected shot humming through the air ahead, and in an instant it was cracking and smashing the branches in the forest beyond.

"They will not do that again," he thought; "The next time they will use a charge of grape. I must keep my eye upon the gun; the smoke will apprise me—the report arrives too late; it lags behind the missile. That is a good gun."

Suddenly, he felt himself whirled round and round—spinning like a top. The water, the banks, the forests, the now distant bridge, fort and men—all were commingled and blurred. Objects were represented by their colors only; circular horizontal streaks of color—that was all he saw. He had been caught in a vortex and was being whirled on with a velocity of advance and gyration that made him giddy and sick. In a few moments he was flung upon the gravel at the foot of the left bank of the stream—the southern bank—and behind a projecting point which concealed him from his enemies. The sudden arrest of his motion, the abrasion of one of his hands on the gravel, restored him and he wept with delight. He dug his fingers into the sand, threw it over himself in handfuls and audibly blessed it. It looked like diamonds, rubies, emeralds; he could think of nothing beautiful it did not resemble. The trees upon the bank were giant garden plants; he noted a definite order in their arrangement, inhaled the fragrance of their blooms. A strange, roseate light shone through the spaces among their trunks and the wind made in their branches the music of harps. He had no wish to perfect his escape—was content to remain in that enchanting spot until retaken.

A whiz and rattle of grapeshot among the branches high above his head roused him from his dream. The baffled cannoneer had fired him a random farewell. He sprang to his feet, rushed up the sloping bank, and plunged into the forest.

All that day he traveled, laying his course by the rounding sun. The forest seemed indeterminable; nowhere did he discover a break in it, not even a woodsman's road. He had not known that he lived in so wild a region. There was something uncanny in the revelation.

By nightfall he was fatigued, footsore, famishing. The thought of his wife and children urged him on. At last he found a road which led him in what he knew to be the right direction. It was as wide and straight as a city street, yet it seemed untraveled. No fields bordered it, no dwelling anywhere. Not so much as the barking of a dog suggested human habitation. The black bodies of the trees formed a straight wall on both sides, terminating on the horizon in a point. Overhead, as he looked up through this rift in the wood, shone great golden stars looking unfamiliar and grouped in strange constellations. He was sure they were arranged in some order which had a secret and malign significance. The wood on either side was full of singular noises, among which—once, twice, and again—he distinctly heard whispers in an unknown tongue.

His neck was in pain and lifting his hand to it he found it horribly swollen. He knew that it had a circle of black where the rope had bruised it. His eyes felt congested; he could no longer close them. His tongue was swollen with thirst; he relieved its fever by thrusting it forward from between his teeth into the cold air. How softly the turf had carpeted the untraveled avenue—he could no longer feel the roadway beneath his feet.

Doubtless, despite his suffering, he had fallen asleep while walking, for now he sees another scene—perhaps he has merely recovered from a delirium. He stands at the gate of his own home. All is as he left it, and all bright and beautiful in the morning sunshine. He must have traveled the entire night.

As he pushes open the gate and passes up the wide white walk, he sees a flutter of female garments; his wife, looking fresh and cool and sweet, steps down from the veranda to meet him. At the bottom of the steps she stands waiting, with a smile of ineffable joy, an attitude of matchless grace and dignity. Ah, how beautiful she is! He springs forward with extended arms. As he is about to clasp her he feels a stunning blow upon the back of the neck; a blinding white light blazes all about him with the sound like the shock of a cannon—then all is darkness and silence.

Peyton Farquhar was dead; his body, with a broken neck, swung gently from side to side beneath the timbers of the Owl Creek bridge.

SUMMARY:

1. Peyton Farquhar, a wealthy Southern gentleman, stood in the middle of the Owl Creek Bridge with a noose around his neck. His executioners stood beside him; close by was the captain who would give the signal; a sentinel stood at either end of the bridge.

2. One side of the creek was bordered by dense forest. On the other side, midway between the stream and the fort, stood a company of infantrymen.

3. When the captain stepped off the plank he shared with the condemned man, Farquhar would be killed. He watched the swirling stream for a moment, then closed his eyes to focus his last thoughts on his wife.

4. As thoughts of escape played in the condemned man's mind, the captain stepped aside.

5. Farquhar and his wife had been at home when a gray-clad soldier had ridden up to their porch and informed them that the Yankees had built a stockade at Owl Creek Bridge, and issued an order than anyone interfering with the bridge would be executed.

6. Farquhar asked in what ways the bridge could be damaged; that was his fatal mistake. The soldier was a Federal scout.

7. Farquhar plunged downward through the bridge, then into the water of the creek below. The rope had broken. He struggled to free his hands, and came up for air.

8. A volley of bullets pelted the water around him; he dived to evade them, and capture. When he came up again, he found everything around him had taken on a vividness—from spider webs to blades of grass.

9. He floated downstream, accosted by bullets, then by the firing of the stockade's cannon. He watched his enemy reload, and swam vigorously downstream. He was caught in eddies, and whirled round, then dumped him on the forested shore. As a final round was hurled in his direction, he ran into the woods.

10. Exhausted from running, he came to his house. His wife comes toward him, a rustling of woman's garments. Then, all is darkness and silence.

11. Peyton Farquhar was dead, his neck broken, his body swinging from side to side beneath the timbers of Owl Creek Bridge.

THE DIAMOND NECKLACE

By Guy de Maupassant

She was one of those pretty, charming young ladies, born, as if through an error of destiny, into a family of clerks. She had no dowry, no hopes of becoming known, appreciated, loved, and married by a man either rich or distinguished; so she allowed herself to marry a petty clerk in the office of the Board of Education.

She was simple, not being able to adorn herself; and she was unhappy, as one out of her class, for women belong to no caste, no race. Their grace, their beauty and charm serves them in the place of birth and family. Their instinctive elegance, their suppleness of wit are their only aristocracy, making some daughters of the people the equal of great ladies.

She suffered incessantly, feeling herself born for all delicacies and luxuries. She suffered from the poverty of her apartment, the shabby walls, the worn chairs, and the faded stuffs. All these things, which another woman of her station would not have noticed, tortured and angered her. The sight of the little Breton, who made this humble home, awoke in her sad regrets and desperate dreams. She thought of quiet antechambers, with their Oriental hangings, lighted by high, bronze torches, and of two great footmen in short trousers who doze in the large armchairs, made sleepy by the heavy air from the heating apparatus. She thought of large drawingrooms, hung in old silks, of graceful pieces of furniture carrying bric-a-brac of inestimable value, and of the little perfumed coquettish apartments, made for five o'clock chats with most intimate friends, men known, envied and desired.

When she seated herself for dinner, before the round table where the tablecloth had been used three days, opposite her husband who uncovered the tureen with delighted air, saying: "Oh! the good potpie! I know nothing better than that—" she would think of elegant dinners, of shining silver, of tapestries peopling the walls with ancient personages and rare birds in the midst of fairy forests. She thought of exquisite food served on marvelous dishes, of whispered gallantries, listened to with the smile of the sphinx, while eating the rose-colored flesh of the trout.

She had neither frocks nor jewels. Nothing. And she loved only those things. She had such a desire to please, to be sought after, to be clever, and courted.

She had a rich friend, a schoolmate at the convent, whom she did not like to visit, she suffered so much when she returned. And she wept for whole days from chagrin, from regret, from despair and disappointment.

One evening her husband returned elated, bearing in his hand a large envelope.

"Here," he said, "Here is something for you."

She quickly tore open the wrapper and drew out a printed card on which were inscribed these words: "The Minister of Public Instruction and Madame George Ramponneau ask the honor of Mr. and Mrs. Loisel's company Monday evening, January 18, at the Minister's residence."

Instead of being delighted, as her husband had hoped, she threw the invitation spitefully upon the table murmuring:

"What do you suppose I want with that?"

"But, my dearie, I thought it would make you happy. You never go out, and this is an occasion, and a fine one! I had a great deal of trouble getting it. Everybody wishes one, and it is very select; not many are given to employees. You will see the official world there."

She looked at him with an irritated eye and declared impatiently, "What do you suppose I have to wear to such a thing as that?"

He had not thought of that, and stammered, "Why, the dress you wear when we go to the theater. It seems very pretty to me."

Two great tears fell slowly from the corners of her eyes toward the corners of her mouth. He was silent, stupefied, in dismay, at the sight of his wife weeping, and said, "What is the matter? What is the matter?"

By a violent effort, she had controlled her vexation and responded in a calm voice, wiping her moist checks. "Nothing. Only I have no dress and consequently I cannot go to this affair. Give your card to some colleague whose wife is better fitted than I."

He was grieved, but answered, "Let us see, Matilda. How much would a suitable costume cost, something that would serve for other occasions, something very simple?"

She reflected for some seconds, making estimates and thinking of a sum that she could ask for without bringing with it an immediate refusal and a frightened exclamation from the economical clerk. Finally she said in a hesitating voice, "I cannot tell exactly, but it seems to me that four hundred francs ought to cover it."

He turned a little pale, for he had saved just this sum to buy a gun that he might be able to join some hunting parties the next summer, on the plains at Nanterre, with some friends who went to shoot larks up there on Sundays. Nevertheless, he said, "Very well. I will give you four hundred francs. But try to have a pretty dress."

The day of the ball approached and Mme. Loisel seemed sad and anxious. Nevertheless, her dress was nearly ready. Her husband said to her one evening, "What is the matter with you? You have acted strangely for two or three days."

She responded, "I am vexed not to have a jewel, not one stone, nothing to adorn myself with. I shall have a poverty-laden look. I would prefer not to go to this party."

He replied, "You can wear some natural flowers. At this season they look very *chic*. For ten francs you can have two or three magnificent roses."

She was not convinced. "No," she replied, "There is nothing more humiliating than to have a shabby air in the midst of rich women."

Then her husband cried out, "How stupid we are! Go and find your friend Mrs. Forestier and ask her to lend you her jewels. You are well enough acquainted with her to do this."

She uttered a cry of joy: "It's true! I had not thought of that."

The next day she took herself to her friend's house and related her story of distress. Mrs. Forestier went to her closet with the glass doors, took out a large jewelcase, brought it, opened it and said, "Choose, my dear."

She saw at first some bracelets, then a collar of pearls, then a Venetian cross of gold and jewels and of admirable workmanship. She tried the jewels before the glass, hesitated, but could neither decide to take them nor leave them. Then she asked, "Have you nothing more?"

"Why, yes. Look for yourself. I do not know what will please you."

Suddenly she discovered, in a black satin box, a superb necklace of diamonds, and her heart beat fast with immoderate desire. Her hands trembled as she took them up. She placed them about her throat against her dress, and remained in ecstasy before them. Then she asked, in a hesitating voice, full of anxiety, "Could you lend me this? Only this?"

"Why, yes, certainly."

She fell upon the neck of her friend, embraced her with passion, then went away with her treasure.

The day of the ball arrived. Mme Loisel was a great success. She was the prettiest of all, elegant, gracious, smiling, and full of joy. All men noticed her, asked her name, and wanted to be presented. All the members of the Cabinet wished to waltz with her. The Minister of Education paid her some attention.

She danced with enthusiasm, with passion, intoxicated with pleasure, thinking of nothing, in the triumph of her beauty, in the glory of her success, in a kind of cloud of happiness that came of all this homage, and all this admiration, of all these awakened desires, and this victory so complete and sweet to the heart of woman.

She went home toward four o'clock in the morning. Her husband had been half asleep in one of the little salons since midnight, with three other gentlemen whose wives were enjoying themselves much.

He threw around her shoulders the wraps they had carried for the coming home, modest garments of everyday wear, whose poverty clashed with the elegance of the ball costume. She felt this and wished to hurry away in order not to be noticed by the other women who were wrapping themselves in rich furs.

"Wait," said Loisel, restraining her. "You will catch cold out there. I am going to call a cab."

But she would not listen and descended the steps rapidly. When they were in the street, they found no carriage; and they began to seek one, hailing the coachmen whom they saw at a distance. They walked along toward the Seine, hopeless and shivering. Finally they found on the dock one of those old, nocturnal *coupes* that one sees in Paris after nightfall, as if they were ashamed of their misery by day.

It took them as far as their door in Martyr street, and they went wearily up to their apartment. It was all over for her. And on his part, he remembered that he would have to be at the office by ten o'clock.

She removed the wraps from her shoulders before the glass, for a final view of the herself in her glory. Suddenly she uttered a cry. Her necklace was gone.

Her husband, already half undressed, asked, "What is the matter?"

She turned toward him excitedly, and said, "I have—I have—I no longer have Mrs. Forestier's necklace."

He arose in dismay. "What! How is that? It is not possible."

They looked on the folds in the dress, in the folds of the mantle, in the pockets, everywhere. They could not find it.

"You are sure you still had it when we left the house?" he asked.

"Yes, I felt it in the vestibule as we came out."

"But if you had lost it in the street, we should have heard it fall. It must be in the cab."

"Yes. It is probable. Did you take the number?"

"No. And you, did you notice what it was?"

"No."

They looked at each other utterly cast down. Finally, Loisel dressed himself again.

"I am going," he said, "over the track where we went on foot, to see if I can find it."

And away he went. She remained in her evening gown, not having the force to go to bed, stretched upon a chair, without ambition or thoughts.

Toward seven o'clock her husband returned. He had found nothing.

He went to the police and to the cab office, and put an advertisement in the newspapers, offering a reward; he did everything that afforded them a suspicion of hope. She waited all day in a state of bewilderment before this frightful disaster. Loisel returned at evening, his face harrowed and pale. He had discovered nothing.

"It will be necessary," said he, "to write to your friend that you have broken the clasp of the necklace and that you will have it repaired. That will give us time to turn around." She wrote as dictated.

At the end of a week, they had lost all hope. And Loisel, older by five years, declared, "We must take measures to replace this jewel."

The next day they took the box which had inclosed it, to the jeweler whose name was on the inside. He consulted his books.

"It is not I, Madame," said he, "who sold this necklace; I only furnished the casket."

Then they went from jeweler to jeweler seeking a necklace like the other one, consulting their memories, and ill, both of them, with chagrin and anxiety. In a shop of the Palais-Royal, they found a chaplet of diamonds which seemed to them exactly like the one they had lost. It was valued at forty thousand francs. They could get it for thirty-six thousand. They begged the jeweler not to sell it for three days. And they made an arrangement by which they might return it for thirty-four thousand francs if they found the other one before the end of February.

Loisel possessed eighteen thousand francs which his father had left him. He borrowed the rest.

He borrowed it from friends, asking for a thousand francs of one, five hundred of another, five louis of this one, and three louis of that one. He gave notes, made ruinous promises, took money of usurers and the whole race of lenders. He compromised his whole existence, in fact, risked his signature, without even knowing whether he could make it good or not, and, harassed by anxiety for the future, by the black misery which surrounded him, and by the prospect of all physical privations and moral torture, he went to get the new necklace, depositing on the merchant's counter thirty-six thousand francs.

When Mrs. Loisel took back the jewels to Mrs. Forestier, the latter said to her in a frigid tone, "You should have returned back the jewels to me sooner, for I might have needed them."

She did not open the jewel-box as her friend feared she would. If she should perceive the substitution, what would she think? What should she say? Would she take her for a robber?

Mrs. Loisel now knew the horrible life of necessity. She did her part, however, completely, heroically. It was necessary to pay this frightful debt. She would pay it. They sent away the maid; they changed their lodgings; they rented some rooms under a mansard roof.

She learned the heavy cares of a household, the odious work of a kitchen. She washed dishes, using her rosy nails upon the greasy pots and the bottoms of the stewpans. She washed the soiled linen, the chemises and dishcloths, which hung on the line to dry; she took down the refuse to the street each morning and brought up the water, stopping at each landing to breathe. And, clothed like a woman of the people, she went to the grocer's, the butcher's, and the fruiterer's, with her basket on her arm, shopping, haggling, defending to the last sou her miserable money.

Every month it was necessary to renew some notes, thus obtaining time, and to pay others.

The husband worked evenings, putting the books of some merchants in order, and nights he often did copying at five sous a page.

And this life lasted for ten years.

At the end of ten years, they had restored all, all, with interest to the usurer, and accumulated interest besides.

Mrs. Loisel seemed old now. She had become a strong, hard woman, the crude woman of a poor household. Her hair badly dressed, her skirts awry, her hands red, she spoke in a loud tone, and washed floors with large pails of water. But sometimes, when her husband was at the office, she would seat herself before the window and think of that evening party of former times, of that ball where she was so beautiful and so flattered.

How would it have been if she had not lost that necklace? Who knows? Who knows? How singular is life, she thought, and how full of changes. How small a thing will ruin or save one!

One Sunday, as she was taking a walk in the Champs-Elysees to rid herself of the cares of the week, she suddenly perceived a woman walking with a child. It was Mrs. Forestier, still young, still pretty, still attractive. Mrs. Loisel was affected. Should she speak to her? Yes, certainly. And now that she had paid, she would tell her all. Why not?

She approached her. "Good morning, Jeanne."

Her friend did not recognize her and was astonished to be so familiarly addressed by this common personage. She stammered, "But madame—I do not know—You must be mistaken."

"No, I am Matilda Loisel."

Her friend uttered a cry of astonishment. "Oh! my poor Matilda! How you have changed—"

"Yes, I have had some hard days since I saw you; and some miserable ones—and all because of you—"

"Because of me? How is that?"

"You recall the diamond necklace that you loaned me to wear to the Commissioner's ball?"

"Yes, very well."

"Well, I lost it."

"How is that, since you returned it to me?"

"I returned another to you exactly like it. And it has taken us ten years to pay for it. You can understand that it is not easy for us who have nothing. But it is finished and I am decently content."

Madame Forestier stopped short, and said, "You say that you bought a diamond necklace to replace mine?"

"Yes. You did not perceive it then? They were just alike." And she smiled with a proud and simple joy.

Madame Forestier was touched and took both her hands as she replied, "Oh! my poor Matilda! Mine were false. They were not worth over five hundred francs!"

SUMMARY

1. Mme. Loisel was a lovely young woman of no wealth, so though she felt she would be best suited to high society, she was relegated to life as the wife of a petty clerk to the board of education.

2. Eventually, the young couple was invited to an elegant party, but Mme. Loisel was distressed, for she had nothing to wear.

3. Her husband, wishing to make her happy, allowed her to spend their savings on a new gown. But that was not enough for the wife; she needed jewels as well.

4. Finally, her husband reminded her of a rich friend who might let her borrow some jewels. Mrs. Forestier was gracious, and allowed her friend to borrow a necklace of diamonds.

5. Mme. Loisel was very successful at the ball, and the couple didn't leave until very late. Upon

returning home, however, the wife was distressed to find the necklace is gone.

6. Her husband searched for it everywhere, but could not find it. Finally, the couple decided to go deeply into debt to replace it.

7. Mme. Loisel, once lovely, found her beauty disappearing as she helped her husband toil to repay the debt.

8. They worked for ten years, until the debts were repaid. One day, Mme. Loisel was walking on the Champs-Elysees when she ran into her old friend, Mrs. Forestier. The latter did not recognize her old friend, given her years of work.

9. Mme. Loisel explained the changes were caused, in part, by Mrs. Forestier. She told her old friend what had happened with the necklace.

10. Mrs. Forestier was astounded, and taking Mme. Loisel's hands, said the necklace she had lost was fake, and not worth much money at all.

Explore other titles from ICS BOOKS!